150+ GLUTEN-FREE
FAMILY
FAVORITES

Tami Dillon and Bonnie Root

HARVEST HOUSE PUBLISHERS
EUGENE, OREGON

Unless otherwise indicated, all Scripture quotations are taken from the Holy Bible, New International Version®, NIV®. Copyright © 1973, 1978, 1984, 2011 by Biblica, Inc.® Used by permission. All rights reserved worldwide.

Verses marked NASB are taken from the New American Standard Bible, copyright © 1960, 1962, 1963, 1968, 1971, 1972, 1973, 1975, 1977, 1995 by The Lockman Foundation. Used by permission. (www.Lockman.org)

Cover by Dugan Design Group

Cover photo © cherylvb / Fotolia

Oven temperatures are in degrees Fahrenheit.

This book is not intended to take the place of sound professional medical advice. Neither the author nor the publisher assumes any liability for possible adverse consequences as a result of the information contained herein.

150+ Gluten-Free Family Favorites
Copyright © 2018 by Tami Dillon and Bonnie Root
Published by Harvest House Publishers
Eugene, Oregon 97408
www.harvesthousepublishers.com

ISBN 978-0-7369-7349-6 (pbk)
ISBN 978-0-7369-7350-2 (eBook)

Library of Congress Cataloging-in-Publication Data

Names: Dillon, Tami, author.
Title: 150+ gluten-free family favorites / Tami Dillon and Bonnie Root.
Other titles: One hundred and fifty plus gluten-free family favorites
Description: Eugene, Oregon : Harvest House Publishers, [2018] | Includes
    index.
Identifiers: LCCN 2017060952 (print) | LCCN 2017061862 (ebook) | ISBN
    9780736973502 (ebook) | ISBN 9780736973496 (pbk)
Subjects: LCSH: Gluten-free diet--Recipes.
Classification: LCC RM237.86 (ebook) | LCC RM237.86 .D55 2018 (print) | DDC
    641.5/639311--dc23
LC record available at https://lccn.loc.gov/2017060952

All rights reserved. No part of this publication may be reproduced, stored in a retrieval system, or transmitted in any form or by any means—electronic, mechanical, digital, photocopy, recording, or any other—except for brief quotations in printed reviews, without the prior permission of the publisher.

Printed in China

18 19 20 21 22 23 24 25 26 / RDS-SK / 10 9 8 7 6 5 4 3 2 1

CONTENTS

~

WORDS OF ENCOURAGEMENT FROM TAMI AND BONNIE

May the God of hope fill you with all joy and peace
as you trust in him, so that you may overflow with
hope by the power of the Holy Spirit.

ROMANS 15:13

Tami

"Y ou have celiac disease." There it was. After months of tests and years of various health concerns, I had my answer. The next line was my favorite: "The good news is that celiac can be controlled with a gluten-free diet…"

A gluten-free diet? Isn't gluten in everything that is good and wonderful? A life without chocolate-chip cookies, rolls, French toast? Wait—a life without cinnamon rolls? Say it isn't so! I don't know if I can live without cinnamon rolls!

I had my diagnosis, but I had absolutely no idea how to change from a gluten-loving person to a gluten-free one. Information was scarce, and average grocery stores and restaurants had very few options back then. While it wasn't easy at first, after almost 15 years of living strictly gluten-free, I'm here to tell you it can be done, and it can be done in a way that allows you to have the food you enjoyed before changing your lifestyle. With some simple substitutions, modifications, and creativity, you can do it too!

If I could encourage you in one thing (other than buying this cookbook), it would be to build a support system for *your* gluten-free journey. My husband and kiddos are great sports regarding my various kitchen experiments. My oldest daughter has spent many, many hours in the kitchen with me making "sugar." My husband is the researcher. He finds new restaurants with gluten-free menus and new products on the market all the time. My son is our picky eater, so he keeps me on my toes to try new things. Living gluten free is a family affair. Encouragement and a bit of help will make all the difference to go from livable to enjoyable.

My mom, Bonnie Root, has been a tremendous support and rock throughout this journey. She's always had such a knack for making something delicious out of nothing. She took this gluten-free challenge in stride and has made recipe after recipe a success. We've spent countless hours perfecting our favorite dishes and researching how to make gluten-free food as delicious as possible. We're so excited to join together to share with you some of the wonderful, practical, and "why didn't I think of that" life and kitchen insights we've learned along the way.

And now for the best news of all—yes, there are cinnamon rolls! Sinfully Cinnamon Cinnamon Rolls are in the breakfast section (THE most important meal of the day)!

~

His mouth speaks from that which fills his heart.

LUKE 6:45 NASB

──────────────── *Bonnie* ────────────────

I accepted Christ when I was eight. That same year, my youngest sibling was born, and from that time on, my mother spent many years in and out of hospitals. As the eldest of five children, I began cooking out of necessity. Fast-forward a couple of years. I learned firsthand that God answers prayer in a very real way. Momma was in the hospital, and we were out of money and food. My daddy and I knelt on the kitchen floor and asked for God's provision. A few minutes later, a family friend knocked on the front door, his arms full of groceries. I believe God loves us so much that those groceries were on their way before our prayers were breathed. He wanted us to be blessed by receiving that tangible answer to prayer. I have never doubted his love or grace since that day. Just as the house built on the rock can't be shaken, a child's heart filled with truth will be strong throughout the storms of life.

I am now mother to three amazing, grown children who have given me seven adorable, little love bugs. My husband and I have been married 40 years, so I've been cooking for more than half a…oh, my…well, need I say more?

Since I began in the kitchen learning by doing, I have not always hit every meal out of the park, but I've learned that sometimes our mistakes are just happy accidents and a whole new dish is born. I've also learned that a positive perspective and giving ourselves as much grace as God gives make life a lot more fun.

His grace was never more abundant than when I was adapting to cooking gluten-free meals for my family. Family nights started out being tacos or barbeques in the summer because that limited the possibility of gluten contamination. As we've grown more adept at changing favorite recipes, and as more gluten-free products have come on the market, it has become fun to experiment. You know the adage, "The more life changes, the more life stays the same"? Well…

Our littlest grandbabies now want to stick tiny fingers in everything, so I'm learning all over again how often God smiled and gracefully loved me through my learning curves in life. Those adorable little chubby cheeks asking for their turn to stir make it all worthwhile.

God bless you, friend, for whatever brought you here. We pray you will find love, hope, patience (if you need it), the answers you seek to healthy eating, and some new family favorite dishes that will make your new lifestyle fun and sustainable.

BAKING WITH GLUTEN-FREE FLOUR

What You Need to Know

~

In all our baked goods, you'll notice we make use of gluten-free flour blends. This is because a singular type of gluten-free flour can't stand alone as wheat flour can. By themselves, gluten-free flours don't provide the structure or body needed for baking. They either deflate or spread during baking, and they don't supply a satisfying bite or crumb. Wheat flours supply starch and protein, and so all good flour blends must do the same in a "6 parts protein and 4 parts starch" equation. You can create a flour blend of your own, but usually at much greater expense in both time and money than using one of the prepackaged blends on the market. Unless otherwise noted, we used a 1-to-1 flour blend to replace the wheat flours in our favorite family recipes. A 1-to-1 flour blend supplies the necessary protein and starch combination needed for successful gluten-free substitution. We found some recipes that do not require the 1-to-1 substitution. One of the joys of gluten-free baking is the curveballs that can be thrown at you at any time.

Other thoughts to consider:

- If you choose to make any of our recipes with a different flour blend than noted, it may not turn out the same because various flour blends measure out differently. For example, we found that 4⅔ cups of Betty Crocker Rice Flour blend worked perfectly in one recipe, where other blends we tried needed as much as 6 cups. That's the reason we included the *weight measurement* in these recipes. Have fun experimenting with the blend that works the best for you, but be sure to give yourself grace. Write down next to the recipe what worked and what didn't. Gluten-free baking is a learning experience.

- Try a stainless-steel, digital scale to weigh your flour. It makes it easier to read and measure precisely and helps with easy cleanup later. Although we don't often recommend spending lots on kitchen gadgets, this purchase is a godsend.

- The best way to measure flour is by using a spoon-and-leveling method instead of just digging the measuring cup into the dry ingredients and leveling off. For this method, use a tablespoon or serving spoon and fill your measuring cup, using the back of a knife to level the flour by drawing it across the top. Then weigh it to make sure you fall within a gram of the desired weight. This will give you an amount you can duplicate every time. Wheat flour weighs 125 grams per cup, so that's what you're shooting for.

1

BREAKFAST

THE Most Important Meal of the Day

Plot twist: Maybe eating a doughnut wasn't cheating on my diet. Maybe going on a diet was cheating on my doughnut!

ANITA RENFROE

~

Amish Baked Oatmeal

Apple Spice Oat Muffins

Blueberry Scones
with Lemon Glaze

Butter Pecan Scones

Chocolate Pumpkin
Breakfast Cupcakes

Cinnamon Apple Cider Syrup

Cinnamon Roll Cupcake Muffins

Cinnamon Sugar Glazed Scones

Double Chocolate Scones

Granola Breakfast Bars

Maple Frosting

Raspberry Scones

Sinfully Cinnamon
Cinnamon Rolls

Wonderfully Yummy Waffles

~

[TAMI] Have you ever paid attention to how many breakfast favorites contain gluten? We had no idea until D-Day (Diagnosis Day—the day I found out I had celiac disease), and then suddenly it seemed as though every single thing I wanted contained gluten. To add insult to injury, my favorite meal of the day is *breakfast*!

Even when you're working hard to eat healthily and choose oatmeal, it needs to be certified gluten-free to be safe. And then it also needs to be handled correctly to stay that way. We will give you some of our favorite hacks, tips, and tricks to enjoy some of your former favorites but gluten-free!

AMISH BAKED OATMEAL

[BONNIE] This oatmeal is a lovely make-ahead, time-saving recipe you can prepare the night before and reheat in the microwave. It will keep in the refrigerator a few days, and thus could save you time several mornings in a row.

We used to make a dish we called fried oatmeal that was leftover oatmeal we refrigerated, fried the next morning, and served with butter and maple syrup. This is a healthier and less messy version of that. Serve with fresh fruit and have a great start to your day.

4 large eggs

1 cup brown sugar

2 tsp. baking powder

½ tsp. salt

1 T. cinnamon

2 tsp. vanilla

2 cups milk

½ cup butter, melted

6 cups gluten-free rolled oats

1 cup chunky applesauce (optional)

½ cup raisins (optional)

Preheat the oven to 350°. Prepare a 13 x 9-inch baking dish with gluten-free, nonstick cooking spray.

In a large bowl, beat the eggs and then whisk in the brown sugar, baking powder, salt, cinnamon, vanilla, milk, and butter, mixing well. Stir in the oats. Add optional ingredients if desired.

Pour the mixture into the prepared pan, spreading evenly. Bake for 40 to 45 minutes. Serve warm or allow to cool completely, Cover, and place in the refrigerator to reheat later.

Serves 12.

APPLE SPICE OAT MUFFINS

[BONNIE] Fall has been my favorite time of year since I was a young child. I love the mix of applesauce and spices in these muffins because they remind me of a delicious applesauce cake my mother used to make. I try hard to make muffins that are loaded with flavor and good things for little people so that someday they might have special memories around the family table.

3 cups (375 grams) gluten-free 1-to-1 flour blend
2 cups gluten-free oats
2 cups brown sugar, packed
1½ tsp. baking soda
2 tsp. cinnamon
1 tsp. salt
2 cups applesauce
1 cup milk
1 tsp. vanilla
½ cup vegetable oil
3 eggs, beaten
1 cup raisins or dried cranberries
1 cup butterscotch chips (optional)
½ cup pecans, finely chopped (optional)

Preheat the oven to 350°. Prepare a 12-cup muffin pan. (I recommend that even if you use cupcake papers, you still use a gluten-free, nonstick cooking spray on the pan. Gluten-free baked goods tend to be sticky.)

In a large bowl, combine the flour, oats, brown sugar, baking soda, cinnamon, and salt, using a whisk to break up any lumps and completely blend all the dry ingredients. In a separate bowl, mix the applesauce, milk, vanilla, oil, and eggs and then blend the dry and wet ingredients until completely combined. Fold in the dried fruit, butterscotch chips, or pecans if desired.

Pour the mixture into the muffin tin. Place in the oven and bake for 25 minutes.

Yields 24 muffins.

BLUEBERRY SCONES WITH LEMON GLAZE

[BONNIE] These scones contain two family favorite fruit flavors, and together they are rather amazing. If you don't love blueberry and lemon together, you could use a plain sugar glaze for a delicious alternative. We love mixing and matching all sorts of flavors, so have fun and make your own special variation.

Scones

- 2 cups plus 1 T. (262 grams) gluten-free 1-to-1 flour blend
- 2 tsp. baking powder
- ½ tsp. baking soda
- 1 cup sugar
- ½ tsp. salt
- ½ cup (1 stick) butter, cubed and frozen
- ½ cup buttermilk or evaporated milk, very cold
- 1 egg
- 1 tsp. vanilla
- 1¼ cups blueberries
- Zest of 1 lemon (optional)

Glaze

- 1 cup powdered sugar
- 3 T. fresh lemon juice or milk (see directions)
- 1 tsp. lemon zest or vanilla (optional)

Preheat the oven to 400°. Prepare a large cookie sheet by covering it with foil and spraying it with gluten-free cooking spray.

In a large mixing bowl, combine 2 cups of flour, baking powder, baking soda, sugar, and salt, using a whisk to mix them thoroughly and making sure there are no lumps. Remove the butter cubes from freezer and cut them into the dry ingredients with pastry cutter until you have crumbles resembling cornmeal.

Place the milk, egg, and vanilla in the center of the mixture and stir with a fork until well mixed with dry ingredients.

In a small bowl, combine the blueberries and 1 T. of flour, making sure the berries are well coated so they won't sink to the bottom of dough. If adding the lemon zest, fold it in with the blueberries.

If the dough is too wet to handle, add up to an additional ¼ cup of flour, a little at a time. Divide the dough into 6 equal parts. Gently roll them into balls, place them on the baking sheet, and carefully flatten to about ½ inch thick and 3 inches wide.

Place in the oven and bake for 12 minutes or until golden brown. Remove and allow to cool for 5 minutes.

While the scones are cooling, prepare the glaze. In a small bowl, combine the ingredients for the glaze, mixing well and adding only enough lemon juice or milk to make it your preferred fluidity for drizzling over the scones.

Serves 4 to 6.

BUTTER PECAN SCONES

[BONNIE] Butter pecan is my favorite flavor of ice cream, so I figured it just had to make a great-tasting scone. Pecan pie and butter pecan scones seem to shout "Autumn!" Stir up some of these yummy scones, make a pot of tea, and curl up with a good book. It's the perfect way to enjoy a beautiful fall afternoon while the little love bugs nap.

Scones

    ½ cup pecans, toasted and chopped

    2 cups (250 grams) gluten-free 1-to-1 flour blend

    1 tsp. baking soda

    2 tsp. baking powder

    ½ tsp. salt

    ½ cup brown sugar

    ½ cup (1 stick) butter, cubed and frozen

½ cup buttermilk or evaporated milk, very cold

1 large egg

1 tsp. vanilla

Glaze

6 T. brown sugar

2 T. water

1 T. butter

½ tsp. vanilla

½ cup powdered sugar

Pinch of salt

Preheat the oven to 400°. Prepare a large cookie sheet by covering it with foil and spraying it with gluten-free, nonstick cooking spray.

Place the pecans in a baking dish and roast for 7 minutes. Remove from the oven and allow to cool. Chop into smaller pieces.

In a large bowl, combine the flour, baking soda, baking powder, salt, and brown sugar, whisking them together to break up any lumps. Cut the butter into the dry ingredients with a pastry cutter until the mixture resembles coarse sand with a few pea-sized chunks. Pour the milk, egg, and vanilla into the center of the bowl and, using a fork, slowly incorporate the wet ingredients into the dry until all are well combined. Fold pecans into the dough.

Divide the dough into 6 equal parts. (If the dough is too wet, add up to an additional ¼ cup of flour by the tablespoon.) Roll the dough into balls between your hands until smooth. Place each ball on the prepared cookie sheet and flatten carefully with your hand until it forms a 3-inch circle about a ½ inch thick. When you've finished the scones, place the pan in the freezer for 30 minutes to chill completely. Then take them from the freezer and place in the oven to bake for 12 to 15 minutes until golden brown. Remove from the oven and allow to cool.

Make the glaze by placing the brown sugar, water, and butter in a small saucepan and heat on low until the sugar dissolves and the butter melts. Remove from the heat and add the vanilla, powdered sugar, and salt, mixing well. Drizzle the glaze over the scones and serve.

Serves 4 to 6.

CHOCOLATE PUMPKIN BREAKFAST CUPCAKES

[TAMI] This recipe is a favorite of mine because it's super simple *and* it sneaks in just a tiny bit of nutritional value my kids aren't aware of. They think they've pulled a fast one on me when they get cupcakes for breakfast.

    1 box gluten-free chocolate cake mix
    1 (12 oz.) can pumpkin puree
    1 tsp. vanilla
    ½ to 1 cup water
    1¼ cups chocolate chips, divided

Preheat the oven according to the directions on the cake mix box. Prepare a muffin pan with muffin papers or gluten-free, nonstick cooking spray.

Pour the cake mix into a large bowl and add the pumpkin puree and vanilla. Mix these ingredients together with a fork or spatula. The batter should be dry and dense. I use the pumpkin can to add water to the batter until it is moist but not runny. Once the batter is the consistency of cake batter, add 1 cup chocolate chips.

Pour the mixture into your prepared muffin pans per the directions on the box. *Optional:* For an extra fun treat, add a few chocolate chips to the top of the cupcakes before placing them in the oven.

Bake according to directions on the box for cupcakes, and until a toothpick inserted in the middle comes out clean. Allow the cupcakes to cool before serving.

These are delicious fresh out of the oven, but they also are great the next day.

Yields 12 cupcakes.

NOTE

One of the things I love about this recipe is that most gluten-free baked goods need to be heated to be enjoyable as leftovers. These cupcakes are great cold a few days later! They are the perfect on-the-go breakfast or snack.

CINNAMON APPLE CIDER SYRUP

[BONNIE] This is such a delicious fall recipe. When the kids were little, we had a favorite orchard we visited every fall for apples and hand-pressed cider. We always used the last of our cider to make this syrup for Saturday-morning breakfast.

1 cup brown sugar, packed

3 T. cornstarch

½ tsp. allspice, ground

½ tsp. nutmeg, ground

1 T. cinnamon, ground

3 cups cider or apple juice

4 T. (½ stick) butter

In a saucepan, combine the brown sugar, cornstarch, allspice, nutmeg, and cinnamon. Then whisk in the cider or juice, mixing well. Cook over medium heat, stirring until slightly thickened. Stir in the butter and reduce heat. Allow to simmer until you're ready to serve, stirring occasionally to keep it from burning. Serve over waffles, pancakes, or French toast.

Yields 2 cups.

CINNAMON ROLL CUPCAKE MUFFINS

[TAMI] Known to most of the rest of the world as Coffee Cake Muffins, this recipe is a fun treat for my family. We all love cinnamon rolls! In fact, when he was a kid, my husband used to ask for them by saying, "Can't we have cake for breakfast, Mom?" While I love our cinnamon roll recipe, I don't always have time to make them. (Sinfully Cinnamon Cinnamon Rolls can be found later in this chapter.) This is a great option to enjoy the flavors of a cinnamon roll in almost half the time. One of my favorite parts is the streusel going through the middle and on the top. As always, if anything is called a "cupcake," even my picky eaters will try it.

Streusel Topping

3 T. gluten-free 1-to-1 flour blend

4 T. brown sugar

1 tsp. ground cinnamon

2 T. (¼ stick) butter or margarine

3 T. chopped walnuts or pecans (optional)

Muffins

1½ cups (188 grams) gluten-free 1-to-1 flour blend

½ cup C&H Baker's Sugar

1¼ tsp. baking powder

¾ tsp. ground cinnamon

¼ tsp. baking soda

¼ tsp. salt

¼ cup (½ stick) butter or margarine

1 egg

1¼ cups buttermilk or sour milk

Preheat the oven to 400°. Prepare a 12-cup muffin pan. (I recommend that even if you use cupcake papers, you still use a gluten-free, nonstick cooking spray on the pan. Gluten-free baked goods tend to be sticky.)

In a small bowl, mix together the first three dry ingredients for the streusel topping. Cut in the butter or margarine until it comes together and resembles coarse crumbs. Add in the nuts if desired, and set aside for later.

In a large bowl, mix together the dry ingredients for the muffins. Cut in the butter until it resembles coarse crumbs.

In another bowl, combine the egg and buttermilk and then add all at once to the dry ingredients and butter mixture. Mix until moistened. The dough will be lumpy and look wet, but that's okay. (Most gluten-free batters turn out best a little moister than you might be used to.)

Fill the muffin cups ⅓ of the way full. Add a layer of the streusel topping (using ½ of the topping), followed by the remaining batter. Finish by adding the remaining streusel topping.

Bake the muffins for 15 to 18 minutes or until golden brown. A toothpick inserted in the center should come out clean. Cool muffins for 5 minutes and serve warm.

Yields 12 muffins.

NOTE

My family likes to top these cupcake muffins with frosting or a glaze for an additional treat. Why not try our Maple Frosting, located later in this chapter? These cupcake muffins keep well in an airtight container. You can reheat and enjoy them later.

~

I used Betty Crocker Gluten-Free Rice Flour Blend in this recipe. Other flour blends will also work but with slightly different results.

~

If you don't have buttermilk on hand, add 1¼ teaspoons of vinegar to the bottom of your measuring cup and then add milk until it measures 1¼ cups. Let this mixture sit while you work with the other ingredients.

CINNAMON SUGAR GLAZED SCONES

[BONNIE] I admit it! I have a passion for cinnamon. Fortunately, it's good for us. These scones are flaky, mouthwatering, and full of lovely flavor. My husband is my guinea pig for baked goods because he isn't a person who overindulges in breads. But when I was working on this recipe, he came into the kitchen and offered to taste test. He finished more than one.

These scones are a wonderful complement to fresh fruit, yogurt, and even scrambled eggs and bacon. What a way to start the day.

Scones

2 cups (250 grams) gluten-free 1-to-1 flour blend

2 tsp. baking powder

½ tsp. baking soda

½ tsp. salt

½ tsp. cinnamon

½ cup C&H Baker's Sugar

½ cup cold butter

½ cup cold buttermilk or evaporated milk

1 egg

Glaze

1 cup powdered sugar

½ tsp. cinnamon

½ tsp. vanilla

1 to 3 T. milk

Topping

2 T. C&H Baker's Sugar

½ tsp. cinnamon

Preheat the oven to 400°. Prepare a cookie sheet by covering it with foil and spraying it with gluten-free cooking spray.

In a large mixing bowl, place the flour, baking powder, baking soda, salt, cinnamon, and sugar, using a whisk to combine all the ingredients thoroughly, making sure there are no lumps. With a pastry cutter, cut in the butter until the mixture resembles sand with varying sizes of peas. Place the buttermilk and egg into the middle of the mix and, using a fork, stir until they are completely combined with the other ingredients.

The dough will be sticky and wet. If needed, add up to ¼ cup flour a little at a time until you can handle the dough. Gather a palm-sized bit of dough and gently roll it into a ball and place it on the cookie sheet. Flatten the ball slightly with the palm of your hand until the dough is a ½ inch thick and about 3 inches wide. Continue creating dough balls and placing them about 2 inches apart on the cookie sheet. Place them in the freezer and chill for 30 minutes. Remove from freezer and bake for 12 minutes.

In a small bowl, combine all the glaze ingredients, adding only enough milk to make it perfect for drizzling over the scones. In another small bowl or cup, combine the topping ingredients, sprinkle over the glazed scones, and serve warm.

Serves 4 to 6.

NOTE

Using really cold butter and milk will make scones, biscuits, and pie crusts flakier and more wonderful.

DOUBLE CHOCOLATE SCONES

[BONNIE] I'm amazed every day by God's love and grace. Some days become miracles simply by the addition of these bits of chocolaty clouds. We all know that a little chocolate lifts our mood and makes some days go a little smoother. I haven't found a Scripture that specifically mentions chocolate, but I'm thinking cocoa must have been one of the wonderful plants in the Garden of Eden. I enjoy apples as much as the next girl but, "Eve, what were you thinking?"

2 cups (250 grams) gluten-free 1-to-1 flour blend

½ cup C&H Baker's Sugar

2 tsp. baking powder

1 tsp. baking soda

½ tsp. salt

½ cup Hershey's baking cocoa powder

½ cup (1 stick) butter, cubed and frozen

½ cup buttermilk or evaporated milk, cold

1 large egg

1 tsp. vanilla

½ cup chocolate chips

Preheat the oven to 400°. Prepare a cookie sheet by covering it with foil and spraying it with gluten-free cooking spray.

In a large bowl combine the flour, sugar, baking powder, baking soda, salt, and cocoa. Stir with a whisk to make sure any lumps are broken up. Using a pastry cutter, cut the butter into the dry ingredients until the mixture resembles coarse sand with varying sizes of small peas.

Pour the milk, egg, and vanilla into center of the dry ingredients. Using a fork, pull the ingredients together slowly until all are well blended. Gently fold the chocolate chips into the dough. If the dough is too wet, you can add up to an additional ¼ cup of flour, 1 tablespoon at a time, until you can handle the dough.

Divide the dough into 6 equal parts. Roll them between your hands until they form smooth balls. Place each ball on the prepared pan and gently flatten with your hand until the ball is 3 inches across and ½ inch thick. Bake 12 to 15 minutes. Remove from the oven and allow to cool slightly.

Serves 4 to 6.

NOTE

Take this treat a step further by adding a glaze. Chocolate, caramel, and vanilla are tasty choices. This is a good way to personalize a recipe to make it your own.

GRANOLA BREAKFAST BARS

[BONNIE] When I was young, we ate a lot of oatmeal for breakfast. It was fast, nutritious, and versatile. Then granola took its place, and we added a whole new level of fun. So much variety: hot, cold, on yogurt, with fruit or alone, in bars and cookies. You name it, we may have tried it. I love how no matter what staples are in our cupboard, we can create something delicious and nutritious.

2½ cups gluten-free oats

½ cup nuts and/or seeds (walnuts, pecans, almonds, peanuts, pumpkin seeds, sunflower seeds)

1 cup sweetened flaked coconut

½ cup dried fruit (raisins, cranberries, cherries, blueberries, apples, pears)

4 T. (½ stick) butter

⅓ cup honey

¼ cup brown sugar

¼ tsp. salt

½ tsp. vanilla

½ cup mini chocolate chips, divided

Preheat the oven to 350°.

On a large cookie sheet, spread out the oats, nuts, and seeds. Toast them in the oven for 3 to 5 minutes (be careful not to burn the nuts). Remove from the oven and put the oats, nuts, seeds, coconut, and dried fruit in a large mixing bowl.

In a saucepan, combine the butter, honey, brown sugar, and salt. Melt together until the brown sugar dissolves. Remove from the heat and add the vanilla. Stir the sweetened butter mixture into the other mixture until it's thoroughly coated. Stir in three-quarters of the chocolate chips.

Press the combined mixture firmly into the bottom of a 13 x 9-inch casserole pan with the bottom of a spatula or cup. Sprinkle the remaining chocolate chips on top and press in enough so they won't roll off when the bars are cut. Cover the pan with plastic wrap and place in the refrigerator until the bars are firm. Cut and enjoy!

Yields 18 to 24 bars.

MAPLE FROSTING

[BONNIE] When my husband and I got married, we moved more than six hours away from our families. Because it was February, my husband worked out in the snow and cold all day. He looked forward to the days when his friends and he would go to their favorite café to get coffee and get warm...and eat plate-sized cinnamon rolls slathered with maple frosting. This frosting recipe is the closest I've come to their signature delicacy. We put our Maple Frosting on our Sinfully Cinnamon Cinnamon Rolls. Tami also puts it on her homemade doughnuts.

½ cup (1 stick) butter, room temperature

1¾ lbs. powdered sugar

¼ cup evaporated milk or light cream

1 tsp. vanilla

1 T. maple flavoring or maple syrup

Cream together the butter and powdered sugar. Gradually add the milk or cream (add just enough to create the spreading consistency you prefer), vanilla, and maple flavoring or syrup. Frost your baked goodies and enjoy.

Frosts one cake or one 13 x 9-inch pan of cinnamon rolls.

RASPBERRY SCONES

[BONNIE] Raspberries are one of my husband's love languages. When we first dated, I was putting myself through school by working at a Dairy Queen and, later, at a restaurant waiting tables. I lived about a half hour from town, and my boyfriend picked me up every night at eleven to drive me home. As soon as I saw him pull into the parking lot, I would make him a ham-cheese-hamburger, French fries, and a raspberry sundae supreme. His birthday is in July, right in the middle of raspberry season, so then and now we have homemade ice cream topped with fresh raspberries to celebrate.

These Raspberry Scones are so wonderful. We all enjoy them. I hope they spell love for someone in your life too.

Scones

2 cups (250 grams) gluten-free 1-to-1 flour blend
2 tsp. baking powder
½ tsp. baking soda
½ tsp. salt
½ cup C&H Baker's Sugar
½ cup (1 stick) butter, cubed and frozen
½ cup buttermilk or evaporated milk, very cold
1 egg
Zest of 1 lemon
1 cup raspberries, cleaned

Glaze

1 cup powdered sugar
1 tsp. vanilla or lemon zest
1 to 3 T. lemon juice or milk

Preheat the oven to 400°. Prepare a cookie sheet by covering it with foil and spraying it with gluten-free, nonstick cooking spray.

In a large bowl, combine the flour, baking powder, baking soda, salt, and sugar. Whisk to completely combine and break up any lumps. Remove the butter from the freezer and cut it into the dry ingredients until it resembles coarse sand with large, pea-sized crumbs.

In a separate small bowl, whisk the buttermilk, egg, and lemon zest together. Pour this mixture into the center of the flour mixture a little at a time, using a fork to stir the liquid into the dry ingredients until all is thoroughly combined. Gently fold in the raspberries.

Divide the dough into 6 equal parts. If the mixture is too wet, add a little more flour one tablespoon at a time, up to ¼ cup additional flour until it can be handled. Roll each part in your hands forming smooth balls. Place each one on the prepared cookie sheet and flatten them into 3-inch circles. (They'll be approximately ½ inch thick.)

Put the cookie sheet in the freezer to chill for 30 minutes. Place the cookie sheet in the oven and bake for 12 to 15 minutes. Remove the scones from the oven and allow to cool for 5 minutes.

In a small bowl, combine the powdered sugar and lemon zest or vanilla. Add just enough lemon juice or milk to make the glaze the best consistency to drizzle over the scones.

Serves 4 to 6.

NOTE

You can get a special tool for zesting a lemon. It resembles a small rasp or plane. You can run a washed lemon over it to remove the peel in little flakes like a fine-toothed grater would. Be sure to not get into the pith, which is very bitter and will counter the lemony flavor you're looking for.

SINFULLY CINNAMON CINNAMON ROLLS

[TAMI] Cinnamon rolls are a big deal in our family. We usually have them when celebrating big events or holidays. My dad used to take each of us kids out for a special shopping trip before Christmas to pick out a gift for Mom and our siblings. During that trip, he always treated us to a Cinnabon. *Sigh!* I can't promise that these cinnamon rolls will make you miss those any less, but they are as close as I've ever come. In fact, my brother-in-law, who loves cinnamon rolls more than anything, requests these gluten-free ones even though he doesn't need to eat gluten-free. (For the best results, follow the instructions carefully.)

Dough

⅔ cup milk, room temperature

1 pkg. RapidRise yeast

2 T. shortening

¼ cup C&H Baker's Sugar

1 egg, room temperature

¼ cup vegetable oil

¼ cup potato starch

¼ cup brown rice flour

1 cup cornstarch

¼ tsp. baking soda

2½ tsp. xanthan gum

2 tsp. baking powder

½ tsp. salt

1 tsp. vanilla

Filling

1 cup brown sugar

1¼ tsp. cinnamon

½ cup (1 stick) butter

Frosting

2½ cups powdered sugar

½ cup (1 stick) butter, softened

1 T. milk

1 tsp. vanilla

Preheat the oven to 375°.

Measure the milk into a large measuring cup and then add the yeast. Use a mixer, emulsifier, or food processor to combine the milk and yeast until frothy and the volume has increased. Set it aside.

In a medium bowl, combine the shortening and sugar. Mix well. Add the milk and yeast mixture and stir. Add the remaining dough ingredients and mix very well. Be sure to remove all the lumps. Scrape the bowl and mix on high for 2 minutes. The dough will be very soft.

Combine the brown sugar and cinnamon for the filling in a small bowl and set aside. Melt the butter.

In your preparation area, sprinkle sugar liberally on the counter. Place the dough on top of the sugared area. Pat or roll out the dough into a large square. (The easiest way to do this is to keep your hands or rolling pin slightly damp with water.)

Spread the brown sugar and cinnamon mixture evenly over the dough, leaving a half-inch or so border along the edge free. Pour the melted butter over the top of the brown sugar and cinnamon. Work the brown sugar, cinnamon, and butter into the top of the dough by hand. Use the edge of a spatula to roll the dough into a long cylinder. (Keeping the edge of the spatula wet will make this easier.) The dough will seem soft or even wet. This ensures a nice, moist cinnamon roll. Use a slightly wet knife to cut even pieces. (To get 9 rolls, make the pieces approximately 1½ inches wide.)

Place the rolls wide-side down on a greased 9 x 9-inch pan. Bake until the tops are light brown, approximately 20 minutes.

While the cinnamon rolls bake, prepare the frosting. Combine the powdered sugar, butter, milk, and vanilla. Mix until all lumps are dissolved and the frosting is light and fluffy. Drizzle over the warm rolls. Enjoy!

Serves 6 to 8.

NOTE

Or try Maple Frosting, my personal favorite!

WONDERFULLY YUMMY WAFFLES

[TAMI] Saturday morning is the perfect day for these tasty waffles, although my family loves being surprised with them for dinner midway through the week too. One of my favorite things about this recipe is that I've tried it with several different gluten-free 1-to-1 flour blends, and I've loved how they've all turned out. This is a great recipe to experiment with. I haven't found a way to ruin it yet! One terrific way to enjoy these waffles is to top them with fresh fruit.

- 1¾ cups (219 grams) gluten-free 1-to-1 flour blend
- 2 T. sugar
- 1 T. baking powder
- 2 eggs, beaten, room temperature
- 1¾ cups milk, room temperature
- ½ cup oil
- 1 tsp. vanilla
- ¾ cup chocolate chips or blueberries (optional)

Preheat the waffle iron.

In a medium bowl, combine the first three dry ingredients.

In another bowl, combine all the wet ingredients. Add the wet ingredients to the dry ingredients and stir until the entire mixture is evenly moist though still slightly lumpy. Stir in the chocolate chips or blueberries if desired.

Coat the waffle iron with gluten-free, nonstick cooking spray or oil. Fill the waffle iron grid one-half to three-fourths of the way full with batter. Close the lid until the waffle is completely baked. (Use the manufacturer's directions on settings and baking time. Our waffle irons take around three minutes on the medium setting.) When the waffle is done, remove, enjoy, and repeat the process.

Serves 4 to 6.

NOTE

For buttermilk waffles, reduce the baking powder to 1 teaspoon and add ½ teaspoon baking soda. Use 2 cups of buttermilk instead of the 1¾ cups of regular milk. If you don't have buttermilk on hand, add 2 teaspoon apple cider vinegar to regular milk to create a similar effect.

~

The waffle iron is one of those places for hidden cross contamination. It may seem silly, but do not use the old waffle iron you made gluten-containing waffles with to make a gluten-free waffle if you are someone who needs to avoid gluten for health reasons. It would be so sad to go to all the trouble to make gluten-free waffles, only to bake the gluten into the waffle with an old waffle iron.

2

BREADS

Baked with Love

Blessed shall be your basket and your kneading bowl.

DEUTERONOMY 28:5 NASB

~

Banana Oatmeal Bread

Blissful Buttermilk Biscuits

Delicious Apple Butter

Mom's Homemade Bread

Pizza Crust

~

[TAMI] Is there anything better than the smell of homemade bread baking in the oven? My mouth is watering even as I consider the question! Okay, homemade cookies also rank up there, but homemade bread? *Sigh…* When you think about eating gluten-free, this is the first place your mind goes. *Bread.*

Let me tell you, I think I've tried every single brand, type, and style of bread on the market, and I'm thankful premade options are available now. But there is just something about homemade bread, fresh from the oven, with something delicious simmering in your slow cooker and music playing in the background. If your mouth isn't watering now, we're here to help. This chapter is full of our most tested and best-loved breads.

BANANA OATMEAL BREAD

[BONNIE] For a bridal shower gift many years ago, I received a cookbook full of old-fashioned recipes I still have 40 years later, even though the cover is long gone and some of the pages have seen better days. One of my favorite recipes for potlucks was the Banana Oatmeal Cake. It looked like a German chocolate cake because of the coconut pecan frosting. This bread reminds me of that cake. To keep it simple for our toddler grandchildren, I don't add the nuts.

- 3 medium-sized, ripe bananas
- 1 cup gluten-free oatmeal, uncooked
- ½ cup (1 stick) butter, room temperature
- 1 cup C&H Baker's Sugar
- 1 cup brown sugar, firmly packed
- 1 tsp. vanilla
- 2 eggs, room temperature
- 1½ cups gluten-free 1-to-1 flour blend
- 1 tsp. baking soda
- ½ tsp. salt
- 1 tsp. cinnamon
- 1 cup raisins, Craisins, or dried blueberries (optional)
- 1 cup mini chocolate chips (optional)
- 1 cup finely chopped walnuts or pecans (optional)

Preheat the oven to 350 °. Prepare two 9 x 5-inch bread pans by spraying them with gluten-free, nonstick cooking spray and placing a rectangle of parchment paper in the bottom of each one (to aid in removing the loaf).

Peel the bananas and place them in small bowl. Mash until smooth. Stir in the oatmeal and allow to sit. In another bowl, cream the butter and sugars together until fluffy. Add the vanilla and eggs and blend well.

In a large mixing bowl, combine the flour, baking soda, salt, and cinnamon, using a whisk to break up any clumps and distribute the spices throughout. Gradually add the creamed sugar mixture. Next add the banana mixture a little at a time until blended. Stir in any optional ingredients you desire.

Pour the batter into the bread pans and bake for 45 to 50 minutes (if you use small pans, you might want to adjust the time or watch the bread more closely) or until toothpick comes out clean. Allow the loaves to cool, run a butter knife around the edges, and remove from pans.

Makes 2 loaves.

BLISSFUL BUTTERMILK BISCUITS

[TAMI] When Mom was a child, every dinner included meat, potatoes, and bread. When she met and married my father, she soon learned that not everyone ate so simply. My dad didn't like biscuits, muffins, or, for that matter, many cakes, pies, or desserts. By the time they had me and then my siblings, most of those goodies were reserved for special holidays or as treats. These gluten-free biscuits are as big a treat as a dessert. Just add homemade jam, apple butter, or honey.

    3 cups 1-to-1 Namaste flour blend
    1½ tsp. salt
    1 T. C&H Baker's Sugar
    1½ tsp. baking powder
    1½ tsp. cream of tartar
    4 T. (½ stick) butter, room temperature
    ¼ cup shortening
    1 cup buttermilk
    1 egg, beaten, room temperature

Preheat the oven to 425°. Coat a cooking sheet with gluten-free, nonstick cooking spray.

In a large bowl, combine the flour, salt, sugar, baking powder, and cream of tartar. Mix well. Cut in the butter and shortening until the mixture resembles coarse crumbs. Mix the buttermilk and beaten egg together, and then add that mixture to the crumb mixture. Using a fork, combine all the ingredients until they are well incorporated.

With your hands, knead the dough until you have a soft ball. Place this on a floured surface. Roll out the dough until it's approximately ¾ inch thick. Using a biscuit cutter or a floured cup rim, cut out biscuit rounds and place them on the cooking sheet.

Bake for 15 to 18 minutes or until golden brown. Remove from oven and serve warm. Yummy!

Makes 8 to 12 biscuits.

NOTE

We tried different flour blends for this recipe, and this one was our favorite. If you don't like the flavor, try making it with your preferred blend. Often doing a recipe again with a different flour makes it your new go-to dish.

~

If you don't have buttermilk on hand, you can put 1 tablespoon of apple cider vinegar in the bottom of your measuring cup. Now pour regular milk into the same cup so the liquid measures 1 cup total. Let this sit while you're working on the rest of the recipe.

DELICIOUS APPLE BUTTER

[TAMI] This delicious apple butter tastes great on our home-made rolls or biscuits, and because it's made in a slow cooker, you can start it in the morning before work and eat it warm with dinner! It also keeps well in the freezer.

10 to 12 large Gravenstein or Granny Smith apples, peeled, cored, and quartered

1 cup brown sugar

2 T. ground cinnamon

½ tsp. nutmeg

½ tsp. ground cloves

2 T. vanilla

Put the prepared apples in a 5½- to 6-quart slow cooker. Mix in the spices and slow cook for 4 to 6 hours.

Mash the apples until they're soft and then mix well. We store our apple butter in canning jars and freezer containers and freeze until we need them. We also make sure we take breaks and enjoy some served warm on fresh-out-of-the-oven bread.

Yields 4 pints.

MOM'S HOMEMADE BREAD

[TAMI] I remember as a child making homemade bread with my mom. The delightful smell wafting through the air still takes me back to those wonderful home-cooked meals. How I missed the enticing whiff of bread baking when I first went gluten-free. But I suffer no more!

Mom's Homemade Bread recipe is not for the faint of heart, but the end result is very rewarding. This tastes as close as we've come to mimicking traditional homemade bread made with wheat flour. And, best of all, the whole family enjoys eating it.

3 pkgs. RapidRise yeast

½ cup very warm water

1½ cups milk

½ cup (1 stick) butter, cubed

4⅔ cups (750 grams) Betty Crocker Rice Flour Blend

½ cup C&H Baker's Sugar

1½ tsp. salt

3 large eggs, room temperature

Preheat the oven to 350°. Spray bread pans with gluten-free, nonstick cooking spray.

Pour the yeast into the half cup of very warm water. Stir and then set aside to allow the yeast to proof. (As the yeast starts to work, it creates a bubbly foam on top of the water.)

Combine the milk and cubed butter in a microwave-safe bowl and heat at 30-second intervals on high until the milk and butter reach between 105 to 115 degrees (approximately 1½ minutes).

Put the flour, sugar, and salt in a stand mixer and stir together. Add the yeast mixture, milk/butter mixture, and eggs. Mix on low, scraping the bowl as needed. After the ingredients are fully incorporated, turn to a higher speed for around 3 minutes until a ball forms.

Lightly flour your preparation area and place your dough on the flour. Knead it until it's smooth and springs back when you push your finger into it (6 to 8 minutes).

Spray a large, clean bowl with gluten-free, nonstick cooking spray and place the dough inside. Cover with plastic wrap. Place the bowl on top of the warm stove to rise until the dough has doubled in size (approximately 1 hour).

Once the bread dough has doubled in size, divide it to fit the bread pans so that they are no more than half full. Cover the pans with plastic wrap and allow the dough to rise again to just above the rim of the pans (approximately 30 minutes).

Remove the plastic and bake the dough for 30 minutes or until the top of the bread is golden brown and the loaf sounds hollow when tapped.

Yields approximately 2 loaves or 22 dinner rolls.

NOTE

While trying to get the dough to rise on cold winter days, set the oven to 150° instead of preheating to 350°. When 150° is reached, turn the oven off and place the dough inside the oven. This keeps the dough warm and helps it rise.

~

DINNER ROLLS VARIATION

Instead of placing the dough into bread pans, shape it into rolls by spraying your hands with gluten-free, nonstick cooking spray and making balls of uniform size. Place the balls into a baking pan and let the dough rise for a half hour or so. Bake for 30 minutes or until the tops of the rolls are golden brown.

PIZZA CRUST

[TAMI] This is one of the first gluten-free recipes I made entirely from scratch after I was diagnosed. We'd go to family gatherings, and everyone else would order pizza (a gluten-free option wasn't available at the time). I read several different recipes and then came up with my own variation after a lot of experiments.

Once gluten-free pizza became more available, you'd think this recipe would be discarded—but my family still requests it! Pizza is a family affair. Everyone gets to add toppings and is usually covered in flour when we're done. Best of all, no one loses interest because the prep time is quick and the food is delicious.

> 2 packets of RapidRise yeast
>
> 1½ cups milk, room temperature
>
> 2⅖ cups (350 grams) 1-to-1 gluten-free flour
>
> ½ tsp. baking soda
>
> 2 tsp. baking powder
>
> 1 tsp. garlic salt
>
> ½ cup shortening

Preheat the oven to 375°. Line a cookie sheet with foil and then grease it.

In a small bowl, combine the yeast and milk until the yeast is completely dissolved. Set aside next to the preheating oven until the volume has almost doubled.

In a stand mixer, combine all the dry ingredients and shortening until well mixed. Slowly add the milk and yeast mixture. Mix at medium speed for 1 minute.

The dough will be wet and very sticky. The best way to handle it is to spray your hands with nonstick cooking spray or keep your hands damp with water. Pat out the dough onto the cookie sheet. For thicker crust, aim for a ¼ inch thickness; for a thinner crust, go as thin as ⅛ inch.

Place your desired toppings on the crust and bake until the bottom of the crust is light brown (about 15 to 25 minutes).

Serves one hungry family of 4.

NOTE

When I combine the yeast and milk, I use my food processor. The result comes out great.

~

This pizza crust can be made ahead of time, baked, and frozen. Then all you have to do is thaw it out, add toppings, and bake it long enough to heat the crust, melt the cheese, and warm up the toppings.

3

APPETIZERS

Let the Party Begin!

The cheerful heart has a continual feast.

PROVERBS 15:15

~

Bacon-Wrapped Green Beans	Little Smokies BBQ Bacon Bites
Craveable Guacamole	Piña Colada Fruit Dip
Deviled Eggs	Smoked Salmon Dip
Dill Pickle Veggie Dip	South of the Border Shrimp Cocktail
Farm Fresh Salsa	Spinach Artichoke Dip
Jalapeño Popper Dip	Sweet Strawberry Salsa

~

[TAMI] In my family, when we gather for dinners, holidays, or girls' night out, we often enjoy fun appetizers. Sometimes we go with old favorites or try new ones and find new favorites. In this chapter, let's do the same thing as we look for ways to celebrate and lighten the cares of the world with a little cheer and silliness. You can never be too happy or share enough with people you treasure. We hope these recipes will give you a cheerful heart and a continual feast.

BACON-WRAPPED GREEN BEANS

[BONNIE] We love green beans, which is amazing because as a teen I spent every summer picking beans to earn money. Anyone else have that "pleasure"? Thankfully, green beans taste great, so that covers a multitude of achy memories. This version is a showstopper! It goes well with Cedar Plank Salmon, Thanksgiving turkey, and Christmas party appetizers.

Green Beans and Bacon

    16 slices bacon

    2 lbs. fresh green beans, washed and tipped

    Salt water

    Ice and water

Brown Sugar Glaze

    ½ cup (1 stick) butter

    1 cup brown sugar

    ½ tsp. garlic salt

    ½ tsp. gluten-free soy sauce

Preheat the oven to 400°.

Line a large cookie sheet with foil, and place the bacon strips in rows. Put them in the oven and bake for 10 minutes. (The bacon will be partially cooked and pliable.)

While the bacon is cooking, clean the beans and then blanch them for 3 minutes in salted boiling water. When you remove the beans from stove, immediately drain them and plunge them into a bowl of ice water.

In a small saucepan, melt the butter and stir in the brown sugar, garlic salt, and soy sauce.

Remove the bacon from the oven and allow to cool. Reduce the oven temperature to 350°.

Remove the beans from the ice water and pat dry. Place in bundles of 5 to 10 beans and then wrap each bundle with 1 strip of bacon. Place seam side down on the cookie sheet. Drizzle all the bundles with the brown sugar glaze. Return the pan to the oven and bake an additional 20 to 25 minutes.

Serves 6 to 8.

CRAVEABLE GUACAMOLE

[TAMI] When my sister was pregnant with her first child, she had major cravings for salty foods—in particular, tortilla chips with guacamole and/or salsa. In fact, she often made that combo an entire meal. But, hey, if that's what sounded good, you go, girl! And because she was constantly thinking about fresh guacamole, I know we'll all soon agree that she perfected the recipe.

½ yellow onion, finely diced

Juice of 1 lime

3 large avocados, mashed

1 jalapeño, seeded, cored, and finely diced

1 clove garlic, finely diced

3 T. cilantro, chopped

1 tsp. lime zest

1 tsp. salt

Soak the onion in the lime juice for 15 minutes.

In a medium bowl, combine the avocado, jalapeño, garlic, cilantro, lime zest, and salt. Stir in the onion and lime juice.

Serves 8 to 10 people.

DEVILED EGGS

[BONNIE] We serve deviled eggs at nearly every BBQ and Easter dinner. (What else do you do with three dozen hard-boiled eggs after the egg hunters are exhausted?) Like many of our recipes, you can experiment and embellish this one to make it your own.

1 dozen large eggs, hard-boiled, peeled, and sliced in half lengthwise

1 cup Best Foods mayonnaise

1 tsp. gluten-free mustard

Salt and pepper to taste

Paprika (garnish)

Parsley (garnish)

Place the eggs in the bottom of a Dutch oven and cover them with cold, salted water. Bring the water to a rolling boil and then reduce heat until the water is gently boiling. Continue cooking for another 10 minutes.

Drain the hot water from the Dutch oven. Cover the eggs completely with cold water and ice and let them sit for at least 5 minutes. Crack and peel the eggs one at a time. (We've found the ice water method helps the shell peel from the egg much easier.)

Slice the eggs lengthwise and carefully remove the yolks. Place the whites on a plate, and put the yolks in a bowl. Mash the yolks and mix in the mayonnaise and mustard. Salt and pepper to taste. Fill the egg whites with the new egg mixture, using generous portions. Sprinkle paprika or parsley to garnish.

Serves 6 to 8.

NOTE

A simple hack for getting the yolk mixture into the egg whites without making a mess is to spoon the mixture into a gallon-sized freezer bag. Snip off the tip of a corner to use as a pastry bag. Piping the yolk mixture into the hollows of the cooked egg whites this way makes the deviled eggs look nice, and cleanup is much easier.

~

A quick note about cross contamination. Peanut butter and mayonnaise are at the top of the list for cross contamination in a kitchen that is not 100 percent gluten-free.

Most people, when spreading a condiment on bread, will dip in with their knife, get a little, scrape it across the bread, and then redip with the same knife, adding bread crumbs to the jar. We've found two easy ways to combat this: 1) buy lots of extra jars to always have a "clean jar" on hand and 2) use squeeze bottles—no knives required. A third, harder, and thus not recommended option is to use a spoon to dish out what you need onto your own plate. Then you use your own utensils on your own food. No matter what, be aware of the risk of cross contamination.

DILL PICKLE VEGGIE DIP

[BONNIE] My grandma used to tell me that when I was a toddler, I would come into her kitchen and say, "Pickles, eggs?" Apparently, ever since I could walk and talk, I've loved dill pickles. To this day they are always in my refrigerator. Now my granddaughters are equally enamored of the lovely little gems, and we add them to any meal we can. This dip, whether used as a chip or veggie dip, will add a dash of pickle love to any spread.

1 (8 oz.) pkg. cream cheese, room temperature
1 (16 oz.) container sour cream
½ tsp. dill, dried or fresh
1 tsp. garlic salt
½ tsp. onion powder
1 cup dill pickles, diced

In a mixing bowl, combine the cream cheese and sour cream, and then stir in the dill, garlic salt, onion powder, and pickles. Cover and refrigerate for at least two hours to allow the flavors to meld.

Yields 4 cups.

NOTE

I don't always have onion powder in my spice cupboard. I recently discovered a gem in the produce section of the grocery store: *freeze-dried red onions!* Tiny little bits of wonderfulness with no tears involved. I subbed them in for the onion powder in this recipe, and they worked great.

FARM FRESH SALSA

[TAMI] Just like the Craveable Guacamole, this recipe was born of my sister's pregnancy cravings. I'm glad my sister had cravings! Using farm-fresh ingredients takes the health value to a whole new level.

1 yellow onion, finely chopped

Juice of 1 lime

10 to 15 tomatoes, seeded, chopped, and drained

1 to 2 jalapeños, seeded, cored, and finely diced (depending on the heat level preferred)

2 cloves garlic, finely diced

5 T. cilantro, chopped

1 T. lime zest

2 T. salt

Soak the onion in the lime juice for 15 minutes.

In a medium bowl, combine the tomatoes, jalapeños, garlic, cilantro, lime zest, and salt. Add the onion and lime juice.

Serves 8 people.

NOTE

Fight the urge to skip soaking the onion in the lime juice. It really mellows the flavor of the raw onion and ensures it won't dominate the flavor of the salsa.

JALAPEÑO POPPER DIP

[BONNIE] I still remember the first time I had a jalapeño popper—it was so amazing! But I couldn't duplicate them gluten-free in a meaningful way—*until* the other day when I found gluten-free bread crumbs online! Now I can't wait for football season to start!

Dip

2 (8 oz.) pkgs. cream cheese, room temperature

1 cup Best Foods mayonnaise

1 cup Mexican-blend cheese, shredded

1 cup Parmesan cheese, grated and divided

½ cup canned jalapeños, sliced

1 (4 oz.) can diced green chilies

Topping

1 cup gluten-free bread crumbs

4 T. (½ stick) butter, melted

Preheat the oven to 375°.

Cream together the cream cheese, mayonnaise, Mexican-blend cheese, and half of the Parmesan cheese. Add the jalapeños, green chilies, and a little of the juice they are packed in (to add flavor and loosen the mixture).

In another bowl, combine the bread crumbs, butter, and second half of the Parmesan cheese. Place the dip into an oven-safe baking dish and then sprinkle with the topping. Bake for 20 minutes and then serve immediately.

Serves 8 to 12.

LITTLE SMOKIES BBQ BACON BITES

[TAMI] This is a great appetizer to share at work or for when you're having people over. What I love is that the basic recipe is simple, so it can be adapted to fit individual tastes. What's also great is that guaranteed gluten-free Little Smokies and bacon are available in any supermarket!

1 lb. Black Label Hormel Bacon (labeled gluten-free)

1 lb. Little Smokies cocktail links

½ cup (1 stick) butter

2 tsp. garlic salt

2 tsp. minced garlic

2 T. gluten-free soy sauce

2 cups brown sugar, divided in half

1 (20 oz.) can pineapple rings, drained

3 to 6 cups Bull's-Eye BBQ Sauce

Preheat the oven to 375°.

Cut the bacon into thirds, creating short strips. Wrap each Little Smokie in one short bacon slice and place seam side down in a large glass baking dish.

Melt the butter in a microwave-safe dish. Once it's melted, whisk in the garlic salt, minced garlic, soy sauce, and 1 cup of the brown sugar. Drizzle half the glaze over the bacon-wrapped sausages. Sprinkle half of the remaining cup of brown sugar over the sausages. Set aside.

Cover the bottom of another glass baking dish with the pineapple slices. Drizzle the pineapple with the remaining glaze and top with the last of the brown sugar.

Put both pans in the oven and bake for 20 minutes. Increase the oven temperature to 400° and bake an additional 5 to 10 minutes or until the bacon is crisped and pineapple is caramelized.

Remove from the oven and place the sausages and pineapple rings on a serving platter alongside a dish of the BBQ sauce dip. Then get out of the way!

Serves 10 to 15 people.

PIÑA COLADA FRUIT DIP

[BONNIE] When I was a teenager and got bored with normal fare, I would open the cupboards and search for things I thought might go together. I wanted to create something new. Sometimes it worked and was a hit; other times, not so much. But the experience gave me the confidence to continue experimenting, so when I needed something special and had no idea what to make, I was able to trust my instincts. Piña Colada Fruit Dip was born from one of those moments.

3 (8 oz.) pkgs. cream cheese, room temperature

1 (14 oz.) can sweetened condensed milk

½ cup C&H Baker's Sugar

2 cups pineapple tidbits, drained

Sweetened flaked coconut

1 (12 oz.) carton extra-creamy whipped topping

In a large bowl, cream together the cream cheese, condensed milk, and sugar until well combined. Using a spatula, fold in the remaining ingredients. Refrigerate for at least two hours so the flavors come together.

Use as a dip for fresh fruit or as part of the filling for a tropical trifle. You can make the Old-Fashioned White Cake and Vanilla Pudding recipes in this cookbook and perhaps add more pineapple. Experiment! Have fun!

Yields 4 cups.

SMOKED SALMON DIP

[BONNIE] This dip has been a family favorite for years. We've always loved seafood, and smoked salmon is at the top of our list. Serve with your favorite gluten-free crackers, and it will be a showstopper.

½ cup Best Foods mayonnaise

1 (8 oz.) pkg. cream cheese, room temperature

1 tsp. fresh lemon juice

1 T. red onion, diced small

1 T. garlic salt

1 T. seasoned salt

4 oz. smoked salmon, chopped coarsely

Place all of the ingredients in bowl of food processor and pulse until mixed well. Spoon into a dip bowl and chill until time to serve.

Yields 3½ cups.

SOUTH OF THE BORDER SHRIMP COCKTAIL

[BONNIE] I used to work with a very sweet friend from Ecuador, and she made this appetizer for special luncheons. It can be a lovely way to wind down after a hard day or week, or it can be the perfect addition to a football spread or holiday party. Make it, and start making some fun memories!

3 Roma or plum tomatoes, seeded and diced

½ cup red onion, diced

⅓ cup cilantro, washed and chopped

1 jalapeño, seeded and diced

2 limes, juiced

Zest of 1 lime

Salt

1 (12 oz.) jar cocktail sauce

1 lb. cooked shrimp, diced

2 avocados, diced

Tortilla chips

Combine all of the ingredients in a large mixing bowl *except* for the avocado and tortilla chips. Place the mixture in the refrigerator for the flavors to meld.

Just before serving the salad, add the avocado to the bowl and mix. Serve with warm tortilla chips.

Serves 6 to 12.

SPINACH ARTICHOKE DIP

[BONNIE] We love this dip! We enjoy it in the fall with other snack foods while we cheer on our favorite football teams. Just getting the family together is fun, but when we serve great food, delightful memories are in the making.

2 cups Parmesan cheese, shredded

1 (10 oz.) box frozen spinach, thawed and drained well

1 (14 oz.) jar marinated artichoke hearts, drained and chopped

2 tsp. garlic, minced

⅔ cup sour cream

1 (8 oz.) pkg. cream cheese, room temperature

½ cup Best Foods mayonnaise

Preheat the oven to 375°. Prepare an 8 x 8-inch baking dish by spraying it with gluten-free, nonstick cooking spray.

In a large bowl, mix together the Parmesan cheese, spinach (make sure all the water has been squeezed out), and artichoke hearts.

In another bowl, combine the garlic, sour cream, cream cheese, and mayonnaise. Then combine both mixtures and place in the baking dish. Put into the oven and bake for 25 minutes or until hot and bubbly.

Serves 8.

SWEET STRAWBERRY SALSA

[BONNIE] I made this salsa for a breakfast picnic during Teacher Appreciation Week a few years ago. I served it with homemade cinnamon-sugar-coated tortilla chips. It was the perfect festive-but-unexpected touch for our special gathering.

Fruit/Vegetable Mixture

2½ cups fresh strawberries, finely chopped

2 cups Granny Smith apples, quartered, cored, and finely chopped

1 cup green peppers, finely chopped

2 T. green onions, chopped

2 T. cilantro or parsley, minced

Dressing

2 T. extra virgin olive oil

Juice of 3 limes

1 tsp. lime zest

1 tsp. sugar

1 tsp. salt

Combine the fruit and veggies in a large bowl.

In a small bowl, whisk together the olive oil, lime juice, zest, sugar, and salt. Pour this liquid over fruit mixture, toss gently, cover, and refrigerate.

Serves 8.

4

SIDES AND SALADS

So Good They May Steal the Show

Do not worry about your life,
what you will eat or drink.

MATTHEW 6:25

~

Asian Broccoli Slaw

Avocado Greek Salad

Baby Red Potato Salad

Cheesy Potato Casserole

Chunky Applesauce

Dill Pickle Pasta Salad

Family Fun Pasta Salad

Fruit Salad with Honey
Lime Dressing

It's Not Easy Bein' [Nearly
All] Green Salad

Layered Salad

Mom's Potato Salad

Oven-Fried Parmesan
Green Beans

Oven-Fried Potatoes

Oven-Roasted Vegetables

Penne Pasta Salad

So Good It's Almost
Forbidden Fruit Salad

Strawberry Spinach Salad

Sunday Shrimp Salad

~

[TAMI] Matthew 6:25 is a favorite verse that has inspired me many times during the last several years. While attending college, I was in a public speaking class. One of the assignments was to read a Bible passage out loud. I was struggling with speaking in front of others, and the professor knew it. He suggested I choose the passage that starts with this verse and goes through verse 34. I would earn extra credit for reading it aloud during a church service.

At the time, I didn't understand why this passage in particular and why he was so insistent that I read it in front of the whole congregation. But now I look back and pinpoint it as one of the most influential moments in my entire education. He believed in me and was even in attendance at church the day I read the Scriptures.

To prepare for both reading it in class and at church, I studied what the passage meant. I was asked at the end of my reading what I thought Matthew was trying to convey, and I still remember my answer: "Matthew and Jesus are trying to help us understand that life is going to be hard, but that no matter our circumstances, our heavenly Father loves us and wants what is best for us. We just have to trust him enough to see us through those times. Worrying doesn't make the situation better. In fact, it robs us of the opportunity to find the joy in the moment." Any diagnosis can cause a lot of worry if we allow it, but God can take any circumstance and turn it for our good.

Here I am today sharing recipes to help you live a gluten-free lifestyle. While I would rather not have to deal with celiac disease, I can use my experience and knowledge to help others on their journey. Now that isn't too bad. Even pain has a bright side—often it comes just before healing. We can look for the bright side and the joy in our lives and our kitchens by creating recipes that bring smiles of joy to the faces of our loved ones. We can set the stage for deep, lasting connections.

Now let's turn our attention to the side dishes waiting in the shadows of the main dish. Given an opening, the lowly sides will try to upstage the lead and steal the show.

ASIAN BROCCOLI SLAW

[BONNIE] This salad is fresh, flavorful, and crunchy. You can use our dressing recipe or, to make it even easier, use ⅔ cup of your favorite gluten-free Asian dressing.

Salad

5½ cups broccoli/coleslaw mix

1 cup (8 oz. can) water chestnuts, sliced, drained

2 (15 oz.) cans mandarin orange slices, drained

1 cup pea pods, stemmed

½ cup green onions, sliced

¼ cup honey roasted almonds, slivered

Dressing

2 T. apple cider vinegar

2 to 3 T. gluten-free soy sauce

½ cup extra virgin olive oil

2 cloves garlic, minced

¼ tsp. ginger, minced

Place the broccoli/coleslaw in a large bowl and then add the water chestnuts, mandarin orange slices, pea pods, green onions, and almond slivers. Toss to mix well.

In a small bowl, whisk together the apple cider vinegar, soy sauce, olive oil, garlic, and ginger until the ingredients are well mixed. Pour this delicious dressing over the salad, cover, and refrigerate for one to two hours for optimum flavor.

Serves 6 to 8.

AVOCADO GREEK SALAD

[BONNIE] I love a good Greek tomato salad, and this is a delicious twist with the addition of yummy, creamy avocado. This is a wonderful salad for the summer when the world is too warm to use the oven or stovetop, and just as lovely later when you want something fresh.

Salad

1 large cucumber, cut in half lengthwise, sliced

4 large tomatoes, cut in wedges

½ red onion, thinly sliced

½ cup Kalamata olives

1 large avocado, peeled, pitted, and diced

Dressing

¼ cup extra virgin olive oil

2 T. vinegar

1 tsp. minced garlic

¼ tsp. salt

Place the vegetables in a large salad bowl.

In a small bowl, whisk the dressing ingredients together and then drizzle over the vegetables.

Cover and refrigerate for a couple hours to allow flavors to blend before serving.

Serves 4 to 6.

NOTE

Feta cheese is usually a key ingredient in a Greek salad, but feta is not gluten-free.

BABY RED POTATO SALAD

[BONNIE] Since my childhood, we've always had the family potato salad as a mainstay at all barbeques or summer picnics. It wasn't until I grew older and was invited to friends' homes that I realized people added things to their salads we never did or that potato salad could come without hard-boiled eggs. Now I find myself with an intolerance to eggs and have begun to make potato salads other ways. We love baked potatoes, so here is our salad version.

- 5 lbs. baby red potatoes, washed and halved
- 1 to 2 tsp. salt
- 1 cup sour cream
- ½ cup bacon bits or pieces
- ½ cup red onion, diced
- Salt and pepper
- 1 cup cheddar cheese, shredded (optional)
- 1 cup broccoli florets (optional)

Place the potatoes in a large saucepan, cover with water, and add salt. Bring to a boil and cook until the potatoes are fork tender. Remove from the heat, drain the water, and place potatoes in a large mixing bowl. Put the bowl in the freezer to cool for 15 minutes. (The potatoes will cool without becoming soggy.)

In a medium bowl, mix the sour cream, bacon bits, and onion and add salt and pepper to taste. Add any desired optional ingredients to the mixture. Pour over the chilled potatoes, cover, and refrigerate until ready to serve. We've found that the flavors develop best over time, so we make this dish at least an hour or two ahead of time.

Serves 4 to 6.

CHEESY POTATO CASSEROLE

[BONNIE] This is one of the few casseroles both my husband and children enjoy. Potatoes, ham, cheese…what's not to love? This dish has been a longtime family favorite. In fact, it's something my mother used to take to church potlucks, and I make it for big gatherings myself. Most often, though, we enjoy it after the holidays when we have leftover ham, or on a cold winter evening when comfort food is the perfect dinner choice.

2 T. (¼ stick) butter

6 large russet potatoes, scrubbed and thinly sliced

1 cup half-and-half

1 cup heavy cream

2 T. cornstarch

1 T. minced garlic (fresh or dried)

1 tsp. salt

Pepper to taste

2 cups ham, diced

2 cups cheddar cheese, grated

Preheat the oven to 400°.

Melt the butter in the bottom of a large baking pan and then layer the potatoes in the pan.

In a bowl, combine the half-and-half, heavy cream, and cornstarch, whisking until all the lumps are gone. Then add the garlic, salt, and pepper, whisking again until everything is incorporated.

Pour the cream mixture over the potatoes and add the ham and cheese, stirring carefully to combine. Cover with foil and bake for 35 minutes, then uncover and bake for 15 minutes more or until golden brown.

Serves 8 to 10.

CHUNKY APPLESAUCE

[BONNIE] Have you ever climbed into an apple tree, hid among its leaves, and eaten an apple straight from the branches? My grandparents had two Gravenstein apple trees, a pie cherry tree, two sweet cherry trees, and two filbert trees. The apple trees were lovely and huge, and the fruit was so delicious that even when they weren't quite ripe, I could not resist. When they finally ripened, we were allowed to pick to our heart's content. Then we spent the day making and canning enough applesauce for our large family. Now with microwaves and tools that core, peel, and slice apples, we make it and serve it warm minutes later. Always a holiday favorite.

    10 to 12 large Granny Smith or Gravenstein apples,
        peeled, cored, and quartered
    3 large cinnamon sticks
    1 cup C&H Baker's Sugar
    Cinnamon to taste

Place the apple quarters and cinnamon sticks in a large, microwave-safe bowl and cover with plastic wrap. Poke a small hole in the middle of the plastic wrap to vent and then place in microwave oven and cook for 20 minutes on high.

Remove from microwave, take off plastic, and then retrieve and discard the cinnamon sticks. Use a potato masher to mash the apples to your preferred texture. Stir in the sugar and cinnamon. Taste and adjust spice levels to your preference.

Serves 8 to 12.

NOTE

I don't know if Gravenstein apples are widely available in late summer where you are, but they are heavenly as applesauce, in a pie, or just eating raw. Our family waits all summer for them, and then we go a little wild making all kinds of dishes to use them in because they have a very short shelf life. Granny Smiths are the next best substitute for a tart apple.

~

This is a wonderful dish that can be prepared in a slow cooker as well. Put all the ingredients together in a slow cooker and let it cook on low for 4 to 6 hours.

DILL PICKLE PASTA SALAD

[BONNIE] This recipe was given to us by a sweet family friend who knows how much our little girls love pickles. Since I've loved pickles since childhood, I can identify!

Pasta Salad

1 (12 oz.) box gluten-free Barilla pasta

½ cup pickle juice

2 cups cheddar cheese, cubed

¼ cup sweet onion, finely diced

2 cups cocktail/baby dill pickles, sliced

Dressing

1½ cups Best Foods mayonnaise

½ cup sour cream

1 T. fresh dill, chopped

4 T. dill pickle juice

Salt and pepper to taste

Prepare the pasta according to package directions. Drain the pasta and put it into a large bowl. Add the pickle juice and allow it to sit for 5 minutes. Drain the pickle juice. Add the cheese, onion, and pickles.

Whisk together the dressing ingredients and pour over the pasta mixture. Cover and refrigerate for at least two hours to allow the flavors to meld.

Serves 7 to 10.

NOTE

We have found that gluten-free pasta soaks up dressing like crazy. You might want to mix up extra to have ready if the pasta seems a little dry.

FAMILY FUN PASTA SALAD

[BONNIE] This salad is fun in that you can pretty much add anything but the kitchen sink and it will be good. We have a new generation of picky eaters, so we are constantly changing this up to appeal to more family members. If you have a few in your family, you understand. If you don't have picky eaters but need to live gluten-free, you'll still understand.

1 (12 oz.) box gluten-free Barilla rotini pasta, prepared

2 (15 oz.) cans baby corn, drained

2 (3 oz.) cans sliced black olives, drained

2 cups cheddar cheese, cut into ½-inch cubes

2 cups grape tomatoes, halved

2 cups gluten-free salami, cubed

2 (12 oz.) jars marinated artichoke hearts, drained

1 cup broccoli florets, short stems

1 cup cauliflower florets, short stems

1 cup sweet onions, diced

12 to 18 oz. Olive Garden Salad Dressing (or other salad dressing of your choice)

Prepare the pasta as directed on the package, drain, and rinse in cold water. Place in large salad or pasta bowl. Add to the pasta all of the other ingredients. Toss to combine completely. Cover and chill for 1 to 2 hours to allow flavors to blend.

Serves 8 to 10.

NOTE

We use Olive Garden's bottled dressing because it is readily available, gluten-free, and a product we trust. Feel free to use any gluten-free dressing you enjoy. The same is true with the pasta. The Barilla brand is a family favorite that tastes enough like wheat-based pasta that we don't even bother to say "gluten-free" to warn picky adults.

FRUIT SALAD WITH HONEY LIME DRESSING

[BONNIE] Our family is crazy for fresh fruit salad, and this one is a keeper. It has all our favorite things, and the dressing adds the perfect amount of flavor and keeps the fruit from turning brown. The colors will make you want to smile!

Salad

    1 lb. strawberries, washed and diced

    1 lb. fresh pineapple, peeled and diced

    1 lb. blueberries

    4 kiwis, peeled and diced

    1 lb. raspberries

    2 mangos, peeled and diced

    12 oz. seedless green grapes, halved

Dressing

    ½ cup honey

    2 T. lime zest

    4 T. lime juice

Place the fruit in a large bowl. In a separate bowl, mix the dressing thoroughly, and then pour it over the fruit, mixing gently and carefully. Refrigerate until time to serve.

Serves 6 to 8.

IT'S NOT EASY BEIN' [NEARLY ALL] GREEN SALAD

[BONNIE] Every once in a while, you just need to go with it and be a little wacky, right? I was trying to think of a fun salad we hadn't yet done, and then Tami tried on a T-shirt with Kermit the Frog on the sleeves. A theme was born! I hope you enjoy a little giggle and some green veggies. I apologize if the song "It's Not Easy Bein' Green" keeps repeating in your head. I understand, though. I'm humming as I type.

Salad

1 head savoy cabbage, sliced thin
1 head green cabbage, chopped small
    (think chopped salad)
4 ribs celery, sliced thin
1 bunch green onions, white and green parts, sliced fine
½ cup green olives, sliced
1 English cucumber, sliced
½ cup grape tomatoes, halved
½ cup pumpkin seeds, shelled and salted

Lemon Vinaigrette

¼ cup fresh lemon juice (about 1 large lemon)
½ tsp. Dijon mustard
1 clove garlic, minced
½ tsp. salt
¼ tsp. pepper
½ cup extra virgin olive oil

Place the salad ingredients in a large salad bowl and toss together.

Put all of the dressing ingredients except the olive oil in a blender and close the lid. Blend well. Drizzle the olive oil in through the port on the lid as it is processing until all the ingredients are completely emulsified. Pour over the salad and serve.

Serves 4 to 8.

NOTE

If you want to take the green theme all the way, substitute a lime for the lemon in the vinaigrette—especially if you love lime!

LAYERED SALAD

[BONNIE] This salad is a favorite side dish for us and a must-have as part of any holiday celebration. My mother-in-law brought it to a family gathering some 20 years ago, and it's still something we ask her to make to this day.

Salad

1 large head iceberg lettuce, washed, cleaned, cored, halved, and thinly sliced

1 large sweet white onion, thinly sliced

3 or 4 celery stalks, thinly sliced

1 large green pepper, seeds and ribs removed, diced

1 (10 oz.) bag frozen peas

2 cans water chestnuts, sliced and drained

Dressing

2 cups Best Food mayonnaise

1 T. C&H Baker's Sugar

1 T. seasoning salt

2 tsp. garlic salt

Garnishes

1½ cups cheddar cheese, grated

1 bottle (2.8 oz.) Hormel real bacon pieces

3 tomatoes, diced

3 eggs, hard boiled, diced

Layer the vegetables for the salad in a 13 x 9-inch pan.

In a small bowl, combine the mayonnaise, sugar, seasoning salt, and garlic salt. Spread this over the vegetables, cover everything, and refrigerate for 24 hours.

When ready to serve, sprinkle the top of the salad with first the cheese, then the bacon pieces, then the tomatoes, and then the eggs.

Serves 8 to 10.

MOM'S POTATO SALAD

[TAMI] I've always loved Mom's potato salad. It's simple yet completely says "summer" to my taste buds. It's funny. Mom and I were talking about it, and I didn't realize how her father and my own dad shaped this salad. Because both her father and the man she married didn't care for onions and other typical trappings of summer salads, this basic salad was created. It's the one I grew to love and look forward to.

Now that I have a family of my own, I can make my own version, right? However, I also married a man who doesn't care for some of the added ingredients one normally expects in potato salad. As with all of the recipes in this book, feel free to make them your own.

    6 medium-sized potatoes
    6 large eggs
    1 cup Best Foods mayonnaise
    Salt and pepper

Clean, peel, and quarter the potatoes and place them in a medium-sized pot. Cover the potatoes with water and set to boil until a knife inserted into the center of a potato comes out easily. Remove the potatoes from the heat, drain, and move to a freezer-safe large bowl. Place the bowl in the freezer for 10 to 15 minutes.

While the potatoes are cooking, place the eggs in a small pot, cover them with water, and bring to boil. Once the water is boiling, turn down to medium heat and boil for 10 more minutes. When the eggs are done, remove from the heat, drain, and place in cold water. When the eggs are cool, remove and discard the shells.

Chop the eggs and add them to the cooled potatoes. Mix in the mayonnaise and combine all ingredients. Add more mayonnaise if desired. Salt and pepper to taste.

Serves 6 to 8.

NOTE

One reason Best Foods is our preferred mayonnaise is because it is gluten-free.

OVEN-FRIED PARMESAN GREEN BEANS

[BONNIE] I'm always looking for new ways to serve vegetables, and this dish seems like a great way to get the love bugs to eat something good for them. If you can eat it with your fingers, it's just like French fries, right?

2 T. extra virgin olive oil

2 tsp. minced garlic

½ tsp. garlic salt

1 egg, beaten

12 oz. fresh green beans, ends removed

⅓ cup Parmesan cheese, grated

Preheat the oven to 425°. Spray a cookie sheet with gluten-free, nonstick cooking spray.

In a large bowl, whisk together the oil, garlic, garlic salt, and egg. Dip the green beans in the mixture and then place on the cookie sheet. When all the beans are coated and spread out in a single layer, sprinkle with the cheese and pop into the oven.

Bake 12 to 15 minutes until golden brown. If you want them to be crisper, turn on the broiler for 2 minutes.

Serves 4.

OVEN-FRIED POTATOES

[TAMI] When I first got married, I was constantly trying to impress my husband with all of the different things I could make. His mom, like mine, is a really good cook, and I wanted to assure him I could keep him fed. Unfortunately, he was pretty picky and wasn't a huge fan of potatoes except in the fried form. I thought I'd be sneaky and make oven-fried potatoes. The first time I made them, he didn't really care to try them, but now, nearly 15 years later, they are a staple in our household. This is another easily adapted recipe to match the flavor of your meal. You can also serve it for breakfast, lunch, or dinner.

10 to 12 baby red potatoes, washed

2 T. extra virgin olive oil

Lawry's Seasoning Salt to taste

Preheat the oven to 400°.

Wash and slice the potatoes in half and put them into a glass dish that has been sprayed with a gluten-free, nonstick cooking spray. Drizzle the olive oil over the top of the potatoes and then season.

Bake for approximately 10 minutes, and then turn them over. The potatoes are done when a fork inserted slides out easily.

Serves 4.

NOTE

We love the versatility of this simple side dish. Our favorite seasoning is Lawry's Seasoning Salt, which is gluten-free. (It's a good idea to check even your usual ingredients often.) Have fun adding spices to match the flavor of your main dish.

OVEN-ROASTED VEGETABLES

[BONNIE] We love roasted vegetables, and this side dish is so colorful and smells amazing while it's cooking. It pairs well with any meat you are serving and adds a little fun as well as delicious nutrition to any meal.

4 zucchini, cut lengthwise and then cut into bite-sized pieces

4 yellow squash, cut lengthwise and then cut into bite-sized pieces

2 large red onions, cut into bite-sized wedges

10 baby red potatoes, halved

2 bell peppers, seeded and sliced in wedges

1 pint mushrooms, halved

2 T. extra virgin olive oil

1 T. garlic salt

Coarse sea salt to taste

Preheat the oven to 450°. Line a large cookie sheet with foil and spray it with gluten-free, nonstick cooking spray.

Place the vegetables on the cookie sheet. If it's too crowded, prepare a second cookie sheet or save some of the vegetables for later. (The veggies won't brown as nicely and instead will just steam if the cookie sheet is overcrowded.) Drizzle the vegetables with the olive oil and sprinkle with the seasonings. Roast for 30 to 40 minutes or until brown and fork tender.

Serves 8 to 10.

PENNE PASTA SALAD

[TAMI] This is a simple-but-yummy salad that in our family is gobbled up as soon as it is made. Start it at least 12 hours ahead of time because the salad dressing is formed by the ingredients. We hope you love it as much as we do. This is a great potluck dish, and most people can't tell that it is gluten-free.

2 lbs. grape tomatoes, sliced in halves

2 T. sea salt

1 T. garlic, minced

3 T. extra virgin olive oil

1 (1 lb.) box Barilla gluten-free penne pasta

1 (5 oz.) pkg. Parmesan cheese, shredded or shaved

2 (3.8 oz.) cans sliced black olives (optional)

1 (12 oz.) jar marinated artichoke hearts, drained (optional)

Place the tomatoes in the bottom of a large glass bowl and cover with the sea salt, garlic, and olive oil. Stir gently. Cover the bowl and allow to sit out overnight.

The next morning, prepare the pasta according to the package directions. Drain and cool before placing the noodles in the bowl with the tomatoes and stirring. Fold in the cheese and the optional ingredients as desired. Cover and refrigerate until ready to eat.

Serves 8 to 12.

NOTE

Our family loves olives, and we don't miss a chance to add them to recipes. Marinated artichoke hearts are also great additions when you want something with a little more flavor and spice.

SO GOOD IT'S ALMOST FORBIDDEN FRUIT SALAD

[BONNIE] This fruit salad has been a favorite holiday side dish since I was a young girl. When I turned 16, my mother threw me a grown-up dinner party. I got to invite 11 boys and girls. We dressed in semiformal attire and were waited on by my family. It was a truly memorable evening. This salad was one of the dishes I chose for that special event.

Dressing
4 T. pineapple juice (see pineapple below)
3 egg yolks, beaten
6 T. C&H Baker's Sugar, divided
2 T. (¼ stick) butter
Salt
2 cups heavy whipping cream
1 tsp. vanilla

Salad
2 (15 oz.) cans pineapple tidbits, drained
  (reserve 4 T. juice for dressing)

2 (15 oz.) cans Queen Anne cherries, drained

6 (11 oz.) cans mandarin orange segments, drained

2 cups miniature Kraft marshmallows

Place the pineapple juice, egg yolks, 4 T. sugar, butter, and a pinch of salt in the top of the double boiler. Cook and stir until the mixture thickens slightly, about 12 minutes. Cool to room temperature.

Pour the whipping cream, vanilla, and remaining 2 T. sugar into a bowl and whip until the whipped cream forms soft peaks.

In a large bowl, combine the well-drained fruit, marshmallows, dressing, and whipped cream. Fold together gently, cover, and chill overnight.

Serves 10 to 12.

NOTE

You may know of a similar salad known as "Frog-Eye Salad." Basically, it's our fruit salad with a very small pasta called acini di pepe. We never did this when I was a child, but when my children were little my mother-in-law made the pasta version. You might be able to use quinoa to keep the salad gluten-free and still have that texture. (Prepare the quinoa per package directions, rinse in cold water, and add just before you chill the salad overnight.)

~

My younger daughter wants it noted that she likes this salad best without the cherries.

STRAWBERRY SPINACH SALAD

[BONNIE] This is a lovely salad any time of year—spring, summer, fall, or winter. We love it because it's so fresh and tasty. You can change it up just a little with whatever you can get, fresh or frozen. No matter what type of fruit or nut you prefer, it will still stand up. We enjoy serving this on the Fourth of July and at Christmas because of the beautiful colors.

- 2 T. (¼ stick) butter, melted
- 2 T. brown sugar
- ½ tsp. salt
- 1 cup pecans, halved
- 1 (10 oz.) bag baby spinach leaves, rinsed
- 2 pints strawberries, rinsed, hulled, and sliced
- ½ cup blueberries, rinsed
- 1 pint raspberries, rinsed
- Parmesan cheese curls (optional)
- Gluten-free raspberry vinaigrette (we like Marie's)

In a small skillet, melt the butter and stir in the brown sugar and salt. Then toss in the pecans, letting the mixture cover the nuts to caramelize over medium heat for 3 to 5 minutes. Remove the pecans from the heat and place on waxed paper to cool.

Place the spinach leaves in the bottom of a large salad bowl. Sprinkle the berries and pecans on top of leaves. Garnish with Parmesan curls if desired. Serve with dressing on the side.

Serves up to 8.

SUNDAY SHRIMP SALAD

[BONNIE] When I was young, everyone wore their best clothes to church every Sunday and saved their best meal for Sunday after services. Sunday was all about God and family, and it was comforting. Sunday dinner at Grandma's usually meant ham, scalloped potatoes, and this shrimp salad.

- 1 head iceberg lettuce, halved, cored, and sliced in thin strips
- ¼ to ½ lb. small, precooked shrimp (small tray from the deli will do)

½ cup Best Foods mayonnaise

1 to 2 tsp. celery seeds

Salt and pepper

Combine all the ingredients in a large serving bowl, gently stirring in the mayonnaise until everything is evenly distributed. Add the seasonings to taste.

Serves 6 to 8.

NOTE

We use Best Foods mayonnaise because it is gluten-free. One of the ways we avoid cross contamination is by buying squeeze bottles with flip-up lids. That way no pesky gluten can be left behind by a contaminated knife.

5

ENTRÉES

Dinner Time, Family Time

*If more of us valued food and cheer above
hoarded gold, it would be a merrier world.*

J.R.R. TOLKIEN

~

Apple Cider Pork Tenderloin

Avocado Mayonnaise BLT

BBQ Teriyaki Chicken

Beef and Bean Enchiladas

Cedar Plank Salmon

Chicken Stew

Cilantro Lime Shredded
Chicken Tacos

Corn Tortillas

Creamy Clam Chowder

Lemon Butter Shrimp
and Asparagus

Mmm Meat Rolls

Oven-Roasted Barbeque
Chicken Breasts

Oven-Roasted Lemon Chicken

Pesto Chicken and Pasta

Pot Roast

Roasted Chicken and Vegetables

Roasted Vegetable Lasagna

Sour Cream Avocado Sauce

Spaghetti and Meatballs

Summer Tomato Pie

Taco Lasagna

Tasty Tostada Pie

Tuna Casserole

~

[BONNIE] Some of the times I love most when looking back at my life growing up were when we all sat around the table after dinner, telling stories, jokes, and teaching our father how to sing songs in German. I knew our father pretended some of his ineptitude with foreign languages, but my younger brothers thought he didn't understand what my sister was teaching him. They were silly songs and of little consequence, but our kitchen was filled with howling and leg slapping until everyone had tears of laughter streaming down their faces. Along with the fun family gatherings, we also learned many biblical truths and the beauty of answered prayer around that table.

Fast-forward to having kids of my own. My husband and I worked hard to keep dinnertime a family time. The recipes we share with you hit the mark. Simple-yet-great meals that can be ready quickly when you get home after a long day. We're praying they will help you create meals your families never want to miss. We also hope they give you time in your day for joy.

APPLE CIDER PORK TENDERLOIN

[BONNIE] Just the title makes me wish for autumn and the farm-fresh taste of home-style apple cider. It brings back sweet childhood memories of fields of burnt-orange pumpkins and golden corn, piles of multicolored leaves for jumping in, peals of laughter, and caramel apples.

These days, one of our autumn treks always includes a trip to a local orchard that makes the best home-style apple cider—sweet and full of cinnamon. Refreshing!

Pork

2 to 3 lbs. pork tenderloin

½ tsp. salt

½ tsp. pepper

1 clove garlic, minced

½ cup apple cider

Glaze

½ cup brown sugar

1 T. cornstarch

2 T. gluten-free soy sauce

½ cup apple cider

Rinse and pat dry the tenderloin. In a small bowl, combine the spices and rub into the meat.

Pour a ½ cup of the cider into the bottom of slow cooker and place the tenderloin in it. Cover and turn slow cooker on low. Cook for 6 to 8 hours.

In a saucepan, combine the brown sugar, cornstarch, soy sauce, and apple cider. Whisk together and cook over medium heat for 4 minutes or until it's thick and the sugar has dissolved. In the final hour of cooking, brush the tenderloin all over every 15 minutes with glaze. Remove from the slow cooker, slice, and serve.

Serves 6 to 8.

AVOCADO MAYONNAISE BLT

[TAMI] We've always loved avocado on our bacon, lettuce, and tomato sandwiches, but when you combine avocado with tomato slices, bacon, and lettuce, sometimes you spend more time putting your sandwich back together than eating it. Avocado toast seems to be a trend now, so we decided to try making this BLT sandwich our way.

  1 large ripe avocado, mashed

  ¼ cup Best Foods mayonnaise

  ½ T. lime juice

  8 slices toasted gluten-free bread

  12 pieces bacon, cooked crisply

  3 large tomatoes, sliced

  8 large lettuce leaves

Mash the avocado and then add the lime juice and mayonnaise and mix well. Lightly toast your bread and then spread the avocado mixture on all slices followed by layers of the rest of the ingredients in each sandwich. Put your sandwiches together and enjoy.

Serves 4.

BBQ TERIYAKI CHICKEN

[TAMI] This recipe is a standout in our family. We serve it with potato salad, corn on the cob, and pasta salad. Teriyaki chicken is the perfect idea for barbeque fare instead of hamburgers or hot dogs because you don't have to worry about cross contamination or finding good gluten-free buns. The marinade in this recipe also works great on skirt steak and tri-tip.

  1½ cups Tamari Gluten-Free Soy Sauce

  8 T. mild molasses

  ¼ cup vegetable oil

  1 T. minced garlic

  2 lbs. uncooked chicken breasts, rinsed and trimmed

Combine the soy sauce, molasses, oil, and garlic in a large container with a lid (or you can combine in a large freezer bag for easier storage and cleanup later).

Cut the chicken lengthwise into strips (roughly two inches wide) and place in the marinade. When all the chicken is in the marinade, seal the container. Refrigerate a minimum of 2 hours or overnight.

When ready, remove the chicken from the marinade and barbecue over medium heat until cooked through completely.

Serves 6 to 8.

NOTE

We use Tamari Gluten-Free Soy Sauce because it's one of the few available in our area labeled gluten-free. Many soy sauces on the market contain gluten, so be careful when using it.

BEEF AND BEAN ENCHILADAS

[BONNIE] This versatile recipe can even include leftovers on "clean out the fridge" day. Quick to assemble, it's packed with good flavors to entice even the finickiest among you! (Well, most of them anyway.)

Filling

1 lb. ground beef

1 pkg. gluten-free taco seasoning (we like Ortega)

1 (28 oz.) can gluten-free enchilada sauce

2 (16 oz.) cans gluten-free chili beans, drained (we like Bush's)

3 cups cheddar cheese, grated

10 to 14 corn tortillas

Cilantro, chopped

Toppings

- 1 head iceberg lettuce, thinly sliced
- 2 tomatoes, diced
- 1 bunch green onions, sliced
- 1 large can sliced olives
- Deli-sliced jalapeño
- 1 to 2 cups gluten-free corn chips, crushed

Preheat the oven to 350°.

Prepare the ground beef as directed on the back of the taco seasoning package. Remove from the heat.

In the bottom of a 13 x 9-inch baking dish, pour just enough enchilada sauce to cover the bottom. In the center of a corn tortilla, place a spoonful of meat, one of beans, and a sprinkle of cheese. Roll the filling into the tortilla and place it seam side down in the red sauce. Repeat this process until all the tortillas and/or filling is used. Cover the enchiladas with the remaining sauce and cheese.

Bake for 20 minutes. Remove from the oven, garnish with cilantro, and serve. Have the toppings available so your fellow diners can choose what they'd like for additional flavors.

Serves 6 to 8.

NOTE

You can replace the beef with leftover shredded chicken. If you don't like beans, leave them out. You can add yellow or white onions, chilies, and green peppers to the fillings or toppings. Have fun making this dish your own.

CEDAR PLANK SALMON

[BONNIE] We used to race sailboats all summer. Every Labor Day, one of our favorite regattas served salmon for the final dinner at the end of the racing season. It's something we looked forward to every year because it was always so amazing.

Salmon

Cedar planks to cook salmon on

2 lbs. fresh salmon, skin on

Dressing

1 cup Best Foods mayonnaise

1 T. fresh lemon juice

1 tsp. lemon zest

1 T. garlic salt

Garnish

1 to 2 fresh lemons, sliced

Soak the cedar planks in water for 1 to 2 hours. While they are soaking, mix together the dressing ingredients and cover the salmon with it. Cover the fish with tin foil. Refrigerate until ready to grill.

When ready, remove the foil and place skin side down on the cedar planks. Place the planks on the grill, put the top down, and allow to cook for 20 to 30 minutes or until the internal temperature reaches 135 degrees and the flesh is pink and flaky.

If the planks flare up, spray with water. Keep the grill hood down as much as possible to allow the cedar smoke to permeate the meat.

Garnish with fresh lemon slices.

Serves 6 to 8.

CHICKEN STEW

[BONNIE] On a cold winter's day, this is such a comforting dish. It's a wonderful way to warm up family and friends from the inside out. It's budget friendly and can be made in the slow cooker. And maybe it will help keep you feeling well like its cousin—chicken soup.

- 6 chicken breasts, boneless, skinless, and cut in chunks
- 3 lbs. baby red or gold potatoes, cut in chunks
- 1 garlic clove, minced
- 4 carrots, peeled and cut in chunks about the size of potatoes and chicken
- 1 large onion, cut in chunks
- 4 cups gluten-free chicken broth

Place the chicken and vegetables in the bottom of a slow cooker and cover with the chicken broth. Put on the lid and turn on low. Cook for 4 to 6 hours.

Serves 4 to 6.

NOTE

We leave the onion in large pieces so members of the family who dislike it can easily take it out. Also, because this way they will require the same cooking rate as the other ingredients.

CILANTRO LIME SHREDDED CHICKEN TACOS

[BONNIE] This was one of the first dishes we added to our family taco nights to change up things a little once we knew we could make it gluten-free. Now when we have tacos, we have a slow cooker full of ground beef taco meat and a slow cooker full of Cilantro-Lime Chicken to choose from, complete with a smorgasbord of vegetables and toppings.

- 2 lbs. chicken breasts, boneless, skinless, fresh or frozen
- 1 pkg. gluten-free taco seasoning
- 16 oz. salsa

2 limes, juiced

⅓ cup cilantro, chopped

1 lime, zested

Place the chicken breasts, taco seasoning, salsa, and lime juice in a slow cooker. Cook on high for one hour, and then cook for four more hours on high or six to seven hours on low.

When the meat is cooked through, remove the chicken breasts from the cooker and shred them (I use two forks). Return the shredded chicken to the cooker and let it simmer until ready to serve.

Just before serving, add the cilantro and lime zest. Serve on corn tortillas with all your favorite taco trimmings.

Serves 6.

CORN TORTILLAS

[TAMI] Just imagine, gluten-free, fresh tortillas anytime you want them for whatever meal you might need them. It's true! Although two special tools are recommended on the bag of Maseca corn flour, through trial and error I was able to make equally tasty tortillas by using only a tortilla press. If you love homemade tortillas, this is a good investment for your kitchen.

2 cups Maseca corn flour

1½ cups water

1 to 1½ tsp. lime juice

Preheat a skillet or griddle to medium-high heat.

Combine the corn flour, water, and lime juice. Mix thoroughly for 2 minutes. It should be a soft, damp ball. If the dough feels dry, add teaspoons of water one by one until the dough forms a slightly wet, soft ball that holds its shape.

Divide the dough into 20 equal parts and shape into balls (approximately 1 oz. each). Cover with a damp paper towel to keep the dough from drying out while you're making each tortilla.

When using the tortilla press, line both sides with plastic wrap. Place each ball between the sheets of plastic wrap and press until each tortilla is flat and approximately 5 inches in diameter.

When removing the tortilla from the plastic wrap, peel it off carefully and place it immediately on your preheated skillet or griddle. Cook the tortilla for 30 seconds on each side, turning 3 times for a total cook time of 1½ minutes. Cover the tortillas with a cloth napkin or dish towel to keep them soft and warm.

Makes 20 tortillas.

NOTE

Making tortillas this way takes a little practice. It took me several tries to get the right shape and not ruin the tortilla when I peeled it off the plastic wrap. Expect to make mistakes at first, but keep at it and don't give up. Once you figure it out, it's quick and easy. The kids have fun making them, and it makes them look forward to having tacos, quesadillas, and tostadas.

CREAMY CLAM CHOWDER

[BONNIE] We love chowder, and we've been making it homemade since before we needed to make sure it was gluten-free. Chowder is a staple during the winter and one of our go-to comfort foods when a warm pot of soup makes all the difference.

4 to 6 large russet potatoes, peeled and cubed

4 (6.5 oz.) cans clams, chopped

1 (8 oz.) bottle clam juice (reserving 3 T.)

2 T. cornstarch

1 T. garlic salt

1 quart half-and-half

1 (2.8 oz.) bottle Hormel Real Bacon Pieces

2 T. (¼ stick) butter

Salt and pepper to taste

Put the potatoes in a Dutch oven and cover with salted water. Boil for 20 minutes or until fork tender. Drain and return to heat.

Lower to medium heat and pour in the cans of clams and the clam juice (reserving 3 T.).

Whisk together the 3 T. clam juice, the cornstarch, and the garlic salt. Add this to the potato mixture when it starts to boil. Pour in the half-and-half, stirring constantly until the chowder is thick and bubbly. Add the bacon pieces and butter, stirring until ingredients are combined. Reduce heat to simmer. Salt and pepper to taste.

Serve in cute soup bowls with gluten-free crackers or gluten-free grilled cheese sandwiches.

Serves 4 to 6.

LEMON BUTTER SHRIMP AND ASPARAGUS

[BONNIE] This dish is lovely anytime you can get sweet, fresh asparagus. Shrimp is so versatile, and it accepts the flavors of so many fun dishes, that it is no surprise it's absolutely great here. The fact that both the asparagus and the shrimp roast fast and taste delicious means you can have an incredible dinner prepped and on the table in a matter of minutes.

Asparagus
1 lb. thin to medium asparagus, stems trimmed

1 T. extra virgin olive oil

1 clove garlic, minced

½ tsp. salt

¼ tsp. pepper

Shrimp
1½ lbs. medium shrimp, uncooked, peeled, and deveined

1 T. extra virgin olive oil

I started there. Fortunately, this one worked out and has since become a family favorite.

    6 chicken breast halves, boneless and skinless

    Garlic salt, to taste

    Salt and pepper, to taste

    2 T. extra virgin olive oil

    2 tsp. minced garlic

    2½ cups gluten-free barbeque sauce (we use Bull's-Eye)

    1 cup Parmesan cheese, grated

Preheat the oven to 375°.

Prepare the chicken breasts by rinsing them in cool water and trimming off extra fat. Season to taste and then place them in a 13 x 9-inch baking dish that has been prepared with the olive oil in the bottom.

In a small bowl, stir together the garlic, barbeque sauce, and cheese and then pour over breast pieces.

Place the dish in oven and bake for 30 minutes. Just before serving, add a little more Parmesan cheese on top of each breast piece. Serve with baked potatoes and a green salad, and you have a quick and easy meal.

Serves 4 to 6.

OVEN-ROASTED LEMON CHICKEN

[BONNIE] Just as with many other recipes, this one was born following a long day at work and having a hungry family waiting to be fed. If you make a weekly menu before you go shopping and then stick to it, you are so much better than I am. I used to go shopping knowing what my picky eaters would try and looking for bargains, so some evenings I had to punt. Now things are much easier because there are just two of us at dinnertime, and my husband has become so much easier to cook for as we have grown older.

2 T. extra virgin olive oil

6 chicken breast halves, boneless, skinless, and cleaned

½ cup fresh lemon juice

Zest of two lemons

3 cloves of garlic, peeled and minced

Garlic salt to taste

Salt and pepper to taste

1 cup Parmesan cheese, grated

Preheat the oven to 375°. Coat the bottom of a 13 x 9-inch baking dish with olive oil.

Prepare the chicken breasts by rinsing them and trimming off any fat. Place them in the pan and cover them with the lemon juice, lemon zest, and garlic. Season to taste with garlic salt, salt, and pepper. Roast in the oven for 30 minutes.

Just before serving, sprinkle with the Parmesan cheese.

Serves 4 to 6.

NOTE

Serve this chicken dish with rice, asparagus, or a different favorite side vegetable, and you have a quick and easy meal.

PESTO CHICKEN AND PASTA

[BONNIE] This is a quick dish that can feed a hungry family in as little as 20 minutes if you have a little help from premade items in your grocery store, such as pesto (a 5 oz. container). But it's also quite easy to make with fresh produce and a little more time.

Chicken

6 chicken breasts, boneless, skinless, cut into bite-sized pieces

2 T. extra virgin olive oil

Pasta

1 (12 oz.) box gluten-free Barilla penne, cooked

1 T. garlic salt

1 tsp. salt

½ tsp. pepper

Parmesan cheese, shredded

Pesto

1 cup basil, fresh leaves packed

1 cup baby spinach, fresh leaves packed

⅓ cup pine nuts

½ cup Parmesan, grated

3 cloves garlic

½ cup extra virgin olive oil

Salt and pepper to taste

Sauté the chicken breasts in olive oil, adding salt and pepper to taste. Place the chicken on paper towels to help the oil drain. Set this aside.

Prepare the pasta as directed on the package. Drain and arrange the pasta in your serving dish. Stir in the garlic salt, salt, pepper, and then top with the chicken chunks and shredded Parmesan.

While the chicken and pasta are cooking, place the basil leaves, spinach leaves, and pine nuts in the bowl of a food processor and pulse several times. Add the cheese and garlic and pulse several more times. Scrape down sides of the bowl and then turn on the food processor and drizzle in olive oil until well incorporated. Add salt and pepper to taste.

Stir the pesto into the warm pasta and chicken, sprinkle on a little extra cheese if you like, and serve.

Serves 4 to 6.

POT ROAST

[BONNIE] This is comfort food that has been in our family for generations. Made with red potatoes and carrots nestled next to the roast, you have a meal in one pot. Combine this with homemade rolls or biscuits and enjoy.

- 3 to 5 lbs. beef roast
- 2 T. extra virgin olive oil, divided
- Salt and pepper to taste
- 2 tsp. garlic powder, divided
- 2 tsp. onion powder, divided
- 10 to 12 small red potatoes, halved
- 6 to 8 carrots, peeled, cut to potato size
- 1 yellow onion, peeled and cut into rings
- 1 (32 oz.) carton beef broth (enough to cover roast in slow cooker)

Rinse off the roast, pat dry, and set on a large platter. Pour one tablespoon of olive oil on top. Sprinkle with salt, pepper, 1 tsp. garlic powder, and 1 tsp. onion powder, rubbing them in well. Flip the roast over and do the same to the other half.

Place roast in a slow cooker, arrange the potatoes and carrots around the roast, and then cover everything with the onion rings and beef broth. Put on the lid and cook on low for 6 to 8 hours.

Serves 6 to 8.

NOTE

This recipe used to include cooking wine and French onion soup, but those are so hard to find guaranteed gluten-free that we took them out and added the onions. Delicious!

ROASTED CHICKEN AND VEGETABLES

[BONNIE] The scent of roasting meat and veggies is a hearty, welcoming smell at the end of the day. Even better is how lovely they taste when you whisk them out of the oven and onto waiting plates. If you prep the night before, this dish can be ready to eat in 20 minutes. We make jasmine rice in the microwave to serve with it, and the whole dinner can be done at the same time. Win-win.

> 4 to 6 large chicken breasts, boneless, skinless, and cut in cubes
> 1 red pepper, seeded, cored, julienned
> 1 green pepper, seeded, cored, julienned
> 1 yellow pepper, seeded, cored, julienned
> 1 red onion, peeled, sliced in strips like peppers
> 2 zucchini, sliced
> 2 summer squash, sliced
> 2 cups broccoli florets, stems trimmed
> 4 T. extra virgin olive oil
> Garlic salt to taste
> Salt and pepper to taste

Preheat the oven to 475°. Line two jelly roll pans with foil.

Place the meat and veggies in a large bowl. Pour the olive oil over them and sprinkle on the seasonings. Stir together. Spread in a single layer on the jelly roll pans. Roast for 20 minutes and serve on a bed of rice.

Serves 4 to 6.

ROASTED VEGETABLE LASAGNA

[TAMI] Although gluten-free products have come a long way, we haven't yet found a lasagna noodle we love. But never fear.

This recipe is so good you don't miss the noodles. You can be creative by adding anything you like, including a meat sauce. Due to the high water content of most of these vegetables even after roasting, this dish may be a little watery, but it's still delicious.

1 (16 oz.) carton cottage cheese

2 eggs, beaten

2 cups Parmesan cheese, grated or shredded

2½ T. garlic salt, divided

8 (2 lbs.) zucchini, thinly sliced lengthwise

1 lb. small, sweet peppers, seeded and julienned

1 sweet onion, sliced and separated into rings

2 lbs. baby portabella mushrooms, cleaned and sliced

1 (16 oz.) bag frozen spinach, cooked, water removed

2 (3.8 oz.) cans sliced black olives

Black pepper to taste

2½ T. extra virgin olive oil

2 (22.8 oz.) jars marinara sauce

2 cups mozzarella cheese, shredded

1 cup cheddar cheese, shredded

Preheat the oven to 450°.

Combine the cottage cheese, eggs, Parmesan cheese and ½ T. garlic salt in a food processor and mix until smooth.

Place the veggies in a single layer on two baking sheets lined with foil. Sprinkle with remaining garlic salt, add pepper to taste, and drizzle with olive oil. Using your hands, make sure veggies are coated with the oil.

Place one pan in top third of oven and one pan in bottom third of oven. Roast for 10 to 25 minutes, checking for fork tenderness. Allow to cool until you can layer into a 13 x 9-inch casserole dish. Reduce the oven heat to 375°.

Start the layer by spreading one-third of the marinara sauce in the baking dish and then adding on top one-third of the zucchini "noodles." Next spread one-third of the cottage cheese mixture. Then sprinkle with one-third of the shredded mozzarella and cheddar cheeses. Repeat these layers twice more.

Cover with foil and bake for 45 minutes, uncovering the last 15 minutes to brown the cheese layer on top. Allow to cool at least 5 minutes before cutting and serving.

Serves 6 to 8.

NOTE

Sun-dried tomatoes and marinated artichoke hearts are also nice additions.

~

Some marinara sauces state that they are gluten-free and some do not. Just read the label carefully.

~

We use cottage cheese instead of ricotta cheese because we haven't found a brand of ricotta cheese that is certified gluten-free.

SOUR CREAM AVOCADO SAUCE

[TAMI] This is a quick and easy addition to your family taco night. My kids call it "fancy" when we have this as a side with tacos. Like them, I think it adds a little something special.

½ cup sour cream

1 avocado

1 to 2 T. lime juice

Salt and pepper to taste

Garlic salt to taste (optional)

Put all the ingredients together in a food processor. Pulse until creamy. Serve drizzled over prepared tacos or on the side as an optional topping.

Serves 4 to 6.

SPAGHETTI AND MEATBALLS

[BONNIE] Isn't it funny how, no matter what our heritage, spaghetti is probably one of the first comfort foods we enjoyed as children? Some of you may have loved just noodles, some noodles with cheese, and others loved noodles with tomato-based sauce from the beginning. Our family was no different, so we worked hard to find a great gluten-free noodle. Although we never had meatballs when our kids were little, Tami makes them, and her children love them.

Meatballs

1 lb. very lean ground beef

½ cup Parmesan cheese, grated

¼ cup flat leaf parsley, chopped fine

1 egg, beaten

2 tsp. garlic, chopped

½ tsp. salt

Sauce

1 T. olive oil

¾ cup yellow onion, chopped

1 tsp. garlic, chopped

1 (14.5 oz.) can diced tomatoes

2 cups tomato sauce

¼ cup basil, chopped

Spaghetti

1 (16 oz.) box gluten-free Barilla spaghetti noodles

¼ cup Parmesan, grated

Preheat the oven to 375°. Line a baking sheet with foil and spray with gluten-free, nonstick cooking spray.

In a large bowl, combine the ground beef, Parmesan cheese, parsley, egg, garlic, and salt. Using your hands, mix together the ingredients and then scoop up about 1 tablespoon-sized mounds and roll to make smooth balls. Place these on the baking sheet. Place in the oven and bake for 15 minutes or until cooked through.

Meanwhile, heat the oil in a skillet and cook onion until softened (about 5 minutes). Add the garlic, cooking until fragrant but being careful to not let the garlic burn (about 3 minutes). Add the tomatoes, tomato sauce, and basil and mix well. Allow the sauce to come to a gentle boil, heating through.

While making the sauce, boil water and prepare spaghetti noodles according to package directions. When the noodles are finished, drain, plate them along with sauce and meatballs, sprinkle with the Parmesan cheese, and serve.

Serves 4 to 6.

SUMMER TOMATO PIE

[BONNIE] This is a fun way to use the abundance of your summer garden or the bounty of your favorite farm stand. Although making pie crust may give you heart palpitations or cause you to need to breathe into a paper bag, take heart. All is not lost. Unlike being in Home Ec and being graded on every misstep, it need not be perfect. Just tasty!

Tomatoes

4 to 6 large, vine-ripened tomatoes, cored, peeled, and sliced

Pie Crust

2 cups (250 grams) gluten-free 1-to-1 flour blend

¼ cup C&H Baker's Sugar

½ tsp. salt

1 cup (2 sticks) cold butter, diced (keep in freezer until ready to use)

¼ cup iced water (keep in freezer until ready to use)

Filling

1½ cups Parmesan cheese, grated

½ cup mozzarella, grated

¾ cup Best Foods mayonnaise

1 T. garlic powder

15 baby spinach leaves or fresh basil

Salt and pepper to taste

Slice the tomatoes and place them on layers of paper towels to drain for an hour.

Place the flour, sugar, and salt in a large mixing bowl, whisking together to combine well. Using a pastry cutter, cut the butter into the flour mixture until it resembles small peas. Add just enough iced water to bring the crust together.

Turn out the dough onto a lightly floured surface and knead to bring it together. Divide it in half and pat into two disks, wrapping them in plastic wrap and putting one in the freezer for a future need and one in the refrigerator to chill. After 30 minutes, preheat the oven to 375° and then roll out the dough to ¼ inch thickness and place carefully in the bottom of a pie pan, covering the sides. Score the bottom with the tines of a fork to keep it from bubbling. Make sure the pie crust is evenly distributed around the top edge of the pie pan, and then use the thumb of one hand and the forefinger of the other to crimp the edge.

Bake the pie crust for 30 minutes, checking at the 20-minute mark to see if it looks brown. Allow it to cool slightly. Reduce the oven temperature to 350°.

In a medium bowl, mix together the cheeses, mayonnaise, and garlic powder. In the bottom of the cooled pie crust, spread a layer of the cheese mixture, a layer of spinach or basil leaves, and a layer of tomatoes. Then restart the layers, ending with the cheese mixture and then leaves. Bake for 30 to 35 minutes. When browned and bubbly, remove from oven, slice, and serve.

Serves 4 to 6.

TACO LASAGNA

[BONNIE] We often have just a few leftovers after taco dinners. This dish is the perfect way to stretch those bits and pieces for one more meal with less than half the work. This version allows you to use your slow cooker, so you could even put it together as you're cleaning up the night before—even less work for dinner the next day.

- 2 lbs. ground beef, turkey, or chicken
- 2 pkgs. gluten-free taco seasoning, divided
- 1 (15 oz.) can gluten-free tomato sauce
- 1 cup salsa
- 1 (8 oz.) bottle gluten-free taco sauce
- 1 (8 oz.) pkg. cream cheese, room temperature
- 1 (15 oz.) can of black beans, drained and rinsed
- 4 large gluten-free corn tortillas (see our recipe or use store-bought)
- 2 to 3 cups cheddar cheese, grated
- Sour cream (optional)
- Cilantro, chopped (optional)
- Green onions, chopped whites and greens (optional)
- Olives, sliced (optional)
- Tomatoes, diced (optional)
- Jalapeños, sliced (optional)
- Avocados, peeled, seeded, and diced (optional)

Prepare meat according to taco pkg. instructions (1 pkg.). Set aside.

Whisk the tomato sauce, salsa, and taco sauce together. In another bowl combine the cream cheese, the other pkg. taco seasoning, and black beans.

In the bottom of a slow cooker, spread a quarter of the tomato sauce mixture. Place one of the tortillas over the sauce. Spread one third of the cream cheese mixture on the top of the tortilla and then a layer of meat, a layer of grated cheese, a layer of sauce, and repeat two more times. Place the last tortilla and sprinkle with the last of the cheddar cheese. Put on the lid and cook on low 4 to 5 hours. Uncover, garnish with any of the optional ingredients, and serve.

Serves 6.

TASTY TOSTADA PIE

[BONNIE] This is one of those casserole dishes that can be switched up in many ways to suit the tastes of whomever you are serving. Several members of our family don't like beans, so sometimes we eliminate them, but if you mix the beans in well with the tomato sauce, they may eat them without even knowing.

1 lb. of ground beef, browned and crumbled
1 envelope of gluten-free taco seasoning (we use Ortega or McCormick)
1 can (15 oz.) tomato sauce, divided
2½ cups gluten-free corn chips, divided
1 (15 oz.) can refried beans
1 cup sliced black olives (optional)
1 cup sweet yellow corn (optional)
1 cup sliced jalapeños (optional)
1 cup diced onion (optional)
½ cup cheddar cheese, shredded
Sour cream (optional)

Preheat the oven to 375°.

In a large skillet, brown and crumble the ground beef and then stir in the seasoning. Add 1½ cups of the tomato sauce and mix well.

Crush 2 cups of the corn chips and place them in the bottom of a 13 x 9-inch baking dish. Pour the meat mixture over the top.

In a small bowl, combine the refried beans with the remaining tomato sauce and spread over top of meat mixture. Add any of your favorite optional ingredients and bake for 20 minutes. Open the oven door and pull out the pan, sprinkling the top with the cheese and remaining crushed chips. Bake another 5 minutes or until the cheese is melted. Remove from the oven and serve with a dollop of sour cream.

Serves 6.

NOTE

We look for national brands to use in our recipes so we know they'll be available where you live. We use Ortega and McCormick taco seasonings because they are yummy and gluten-free. We also believe Lays and Mission brand chips are gluten-free as of this writing.

TUNA CASSEROLE

[TAMI] For my bridal shower, my sister and soon-to-be sister-in-law had the guests bring family recipes to share with me. The two recipes I wanted most from my mother-in-law were the only two I knew would really matter to my soon-to-be husband. One of them I'd been working on since I first started helping out my mom in the kitchen: chocolate chip cookies. The second was something I'd never made or eaten prior to meeting my in-laws: tuna casserole. On both of the recipe cards my mother-in-law filled out for me, under how many people the recipe served, she wrote just my husband's name.

When I had to move to eating gluten-free, I was glad we could adapt this recipe so we can both enjoy his favorite dish.

1 (12 oz.) box gluten-free Barilla pasta (we use rotini or penne)

2 (15 oz.) cans gluten-free cream of mushroom soup

1 tsp. Worcestershire sauce

1 tsp. dried minced onion

1 tsp. cayenne pepper

1 tsp. mustard powder

1 tsp. garlic salt

Salt and pepper to taste

2 (5 oz.) cans tuna, packed in water

1 cup peas, frozen

1 cup cheddar cheese, shredded

Preheat the oven to 350°.

Boil the noodles according to package directions. In a saucepan, combine the soup and seasonings. Stir in the tuna, water and all. Add one additional tuna can full of water. Stir together and heat until hot. Microwave the peas for 1 minute, drain, and add to the soup mixture.

Drain the cooked noodles. Add the soup mixture to the noodles, and stir until well combined. Pour into a 13 x 9-inch casserole dish. Cover with the cheese and bake until heated through and the cheese is completely melted, about 10 to 15 minutes.

Serves 1 husband or 6 to 8 people.

NOTE

For noodles, I prefer the Barilla brand. In this dish, they hold up the best to being boiled and baked without falling apart or becoming too mushy.

6

COOKIES AND BARS

The Sweets Dreams Are Made Of

*Better is a dish of vegetables where love is
than a fattened ox served with hatred.*

PROVERBS 15:17 NASB

~

Blond Brownies

Butterscotch Apple Cookies

Caramel Apple Oatmeal Bars

Chewy Gingersnaps

Chocolate Peanut
Butter Goodness

Chocolate Peanut Butter
Rice Crispy Bars

Cinnamon Crackle Cookies

Coconut Chocolate Chip Cookies

Coconutty Chocolate
Brownie Bars

Fruit Jam and Coconut Bars

Homemade Brownies

Lemon Raspberry Bars

No-Bake Chocolate
and Toffee Bars

No-Bake Chocolate
Oatmeal Cookies

No-Bake Toffee
Chocolate Cookies

No-Flour Peanut Butter Cookies

Peanut Butter Clouds

S'mores Cookie Cups

~

[BONNIE] When I read Proverbs 15:17 for the first time, I realized just how much God loves to laugh too. I'd been on a strict diet for nine months, including a cross-country car trip for a weeklong sailing championship. We'd just finished sailing for the day, and the family was digging into homemade cookies. After all those months, I wanted just one…but I also knew I had to separate myself from those cookies. I grumpily went into our tent, grabbed my Bible, and plopped onto my sleeping bag to read. When I sat down, my Bible fell open to this proverb. As I read, the frustration melted away and I laughed. I'm convinced God was laughing right along with me!

BLOND BROWNIES

[BONNIE] Born into a family with dark hair, my beautiful blond, blue-eyed daughter, Tami, took refuge in anything blond that she could. This recipe was probably her favorite before we even made it because of the name. She loved it then and loves it to this day, gluten-free. (And now that we have four little blond boys and three little brown-haired girls in the family, she will never be alone again!)

1 cup (2 sticks) butter

2 cups brown sugar

2 eggs

2 tsp. vanilla

2 cups gluten-free 1-to-1 flour blend

¼ tsp. baking soda

1 tsp. baking powder

1 tsp. salt

1½ cups chocolate chips

Preheat the oven to 350°.

Melt the butter in a large saucepan and then add the brown sugar, blending well. In a medium-sized bowl, lightly beat the eggs and then temper them by adding a little of the buttery brown sugar to them before adding the rest of the brown sugar to the bowl. Add the vanilla and stir everything together.

In a separate bowl, mix together the flour, baking soda, baking powder, and salt. Add the dry ingredients gradually to the wet, mixing well. Spread the dough in the bottom of a 13 x 9-inch pan. Sprinkle the chocolate chips on the top and lightly press into dough. Cook for 30 minutes, remove from the oven, allow to cool, and cut into bars.

Yields 24 bars.

BUTTERSCOTCH APPLE COOKIES

[BONNIE] The flavors in these cookies speak fall to me. They make me think of cozy nights and dappled-sun days. I adore the fall. I have so many memories of family fun and beautiful colors. And the moderate temperatures after the heat of summer are heavenly!

Cookies

2⅓ cups (292 grams) gluten-free 1-to-1 flour blend (we use Betty Crocker GF flour)

1 tsp. baking soda

1 tsp. cinnamon

1 tsp. cloves

½ tsp. nutmeg

½ tsp. salt

½ cup (1 stick) butter, room temperature

1½ cups brown sugar

1 egg, room temperature

½ cup apple juice or apple cider

¾ cup grated Granny Smith or Gravenstein apple

½ cup raisins

½ cup chopped walnuts or pecans

1 (12 oz.) pkg. butterscotch chips, divided

Frosting

4 T. (½ stick) butter, room temperature

½ cup butterscotch chips (reserved)

1½ cups powdered sugar

2½ tsp. heavy cream

¼ tsp. salt

Preheat the oven to 350°. Line cookie sheets with parchment paper.

In a large bowl, combine the dry ingredients and whisk together completely. In another bowl, cream the butter and sugar until fluffy and then add the egg and juice, mixing well. Add the dry ingredients a third at a time until combined. Stir in the grated apple, raisins, nuts, and butterscotch chips (reserving ½ cup of chips for the frosting).

Roll the dough into teaspoon-sized balls and place on the cookie sheets. Bake for 12 minutes.

While the cookies are baking, melt the 4 T. butter and ½ cup of butterscotch chips over medium heat. Add the powdered sugar, heavy cream, and salt, stirring until smooth and spreadable.

Allow to cool completely before frosting.

Yields approximately 4 dozen cookies.

CARAMEL APPLE OATMEAL BARS

[BONNIE] This recipe has been such a wonderful addition to so many family dinners and celebrations, it just had to be shared. We started making it long before it had to be gluten-free, but it was also one of the first recipes we created and adapted. Just like it sounds, it is filled with delicious flavors. We're sure this will become one of your favorites. This recipe is easily doubled. We always do.

    6 Granny Smith apples, peeled, cored, and sliced

    1¾ cups (218.75 grams) gluten-free 1-to-1 flour blend

    1 cup gluten-free oatmeal, uncooked

    1 cup brown sugar, firmly packed

    ½ tsp. baking powder

    ½ tsp. salt

    1 cup (2 sticks) butter, cubed and cold

    1 tsp. cinnamon

    ½ cup C&H Baker's Sugar

    1 (16 oz.) tub caramel apple dip

Preheat the oven to 375°.

Place the apples in large microwave-safe bowl, cover with plastic wrap, and microwave on high for 15 to 20 minutes.

While the apples cook, prepare the crust. In a large bowl, combine the flour, oatmeal, brown sugar, baking powder, and salt. Mix well, and then cut in the butter until crumbly. Reserve 1½ cups of the mixture and press the rest into the bottom of a 13 x 9-inch baking dish. Bake for 15 minutes.

Add the cinnamon and sugar to the apples and allow to cool slightly while the crust bakes. When the crust is ready, remove the baking dish from the oven and carefully spoon the apples onto the crust and then spread the caramel sauce over the apples. Crumble the reserved crust mixture over the caramel layer and return the pan to the oven. Bake an additional 20 minutes or until golden brown and bubbly. Serve warm, topped with homemade whipped cream or a scoop of ice cream.

Serves 10 to 12.

CHEWY GINGERSNAPS

[BONNIE] This is a generational family favorite. When I was little, we used to make these at Christmastime and every time we went to Boise to visit my mother's parents. My grandfather loved them, but my grandmother restricted his sweet intake in an act of love. So we snuck some to him. The two of them played off each other to make things fun for us, I'm sure. It was always fun and a little exciting to *secretly* give Bawpa his favorites.

    ¼ cup shortening
    1 cup brown sugar, packed
    ¼ cup Brer Rabbit molasses
    1 egg, lightly beaten
    2½ cups (312.5 grams) gluten-free 1-to-1 flour blend
    2 tsp. baking soda
    ½ tsp. salt
    1 tsp. ground ginger

1 tsp. ground cinnamon

½ tsp. ground cloves

Extra sugar

Preheat the oven to 375°. Prepare cookie sheets with gluten-free, nonstick cooking spray.

Cream together shortening, sugar, molasses, and egg.

In another bowl, combine the flour, baking soda, salt, ginger, cinnamon, and cloves, using a whisk to break up clumps. Add this mixture to the molasses mixture, combining well.

Roll the dough into small balls and then roll the balls in sugar before placing on the cookie sheet.

Bake for 10 to 12 minutes.

Yields approximately 5 dozen cookies.

CHOCOLATE PEANUT BUTTER GOODNESS

[BONNIE] Chocolate and peanut butter make just about every person in our family happy. The first time I made this dessert, the younger men nearly fought over who got to take the leftovers home. They are the ones who named it, and if I am at a loss for something to make them happy…well, you guessed it. I hope you have someone special to share it with, and that it will make them equally as content. If you love peanut butter cups…this is the dessert for you!

2½ cups powdered sugar

½ cup brown sugar

2 cups creamy peanut butter

¾ cup (1½ sticks) butter, room temperature, divided

1 tsp. vanilla

1 cup milk chocolate or dark chocolate chips

In a large mixing bowl, cream together the sugars, peanut butter, and ½ cup (1 stick) butter. Add the vanilla and mix well. Press the dough into the bottom of a 13 x 9-inch glass baking dish.

In a small bowl, place the chocolate chips and the remaining butter. Use your microwave to melt them together until the chocolate is smooth and creamy. Pour over the top of the peanut butter mixture and smooth it out. Cover with plastic wrap and refrigerate until set or overnight.

Yields 24 squares.

CHOCOLATE PEANUT BUTTER RICE CRISPY BARS

[BONNIE] This is a fun recipe kids of all ages love. You don't even have to have gluten-free marshmallows on hand. Turn a frown upside down with these winners!

    1 cup Karo light syrup
    1 cup C&H Baker's Sugar
    1½ cups peanut butter
    1 tsp. vanilla
    6 cups gluten-free rice crispy cereal
    2 (12 oz.) pkgs. chocolate chips

In a large saucepan, bring the syrup and sugar to a boil. Add the peanut butter, vanilla, and cereal, coating the cereal completely.

Press the rice crispy mixture firmly and evenly into the bottom of a cookie sheet lined with parchment paper and sprayed with cooking spray. Melt the chocolate chips and pour over mixture. Spread out evenly and cover completely. Place in the freezer for 5 minutes to set the chocolate. Remove and cut into bars.

Yields 12 to 24 bars.

CINNAMON CRACKLE COOKIES

[BONNIE] These are a wonderful, light fall cookie that makes the house smell lovely and warms your heart with thoughts of home. The smell or the taste of cinnamon always makes me feel nostalgic. If you love Snickerdoodle cookies, you'll love these too.

½ cup (1 stick) butter, room temperature

½ cup shortening

1 cup C&H Baker's Sugar

½ cup brown sugar

1 egg, room temperature

1 tsp. vanilla

½ tsp. almond extract

2 cups (250 grams) gluten-free 1-to-1 flour blend
   (we used Betty Crocker GF flour blend)

2 tsp. baking soda

2 tsp. cream of tartar

1 T. cinnamon

2 tsp. nutmeg

2 tsp. lemon zest

2 tsp. orange zest

½ tsp. salt

Additional sugar

Preheat the oven to 350°. Prepare a parchment-lined cookie sheet.

In a large bowl, cream together the butter, shortening, and sugars. Beat until fluffy. Add the egg, vanilla, and almond extract and mix thoroughly.

In a separate bowl combine the flour, baking soda, cream of tartar, spices, zests, and salt, whisking to blend everything together and break up any lumps. Gradually add dry ingredients to the wet ingredients and blend until completely combined.

Roll teaspoon-sized balls of dough in additional sugar and place on the cookie sheet. Bake for 10 to 12 minutes and then remove to a cooling rack.

Yields approximately 3 dozen cookies.

COCONUT CHOCOLATE CHIP COOKIES

[BONNIE] These cookies are dairy- and egg-free and still moist and full of wonderful flavor. They remind me of Almond Joy candy bars.

    10 T. coconut milk

    1½ tsp. vanilla

    4 T. C&H Baker's Sugar

    ¼ tsp. salt

    2 cups gluten-free extra-fine almond flour

    1 cup sweetened flaked coconut

    1 cup mini chocolate chips

Preheat the oven to 350°. Line a cookie sheet with parchment paper and spray with gluten-free, nonstick cooking spray.

Because this recipe doesn't include eggs or butter, all of the ingredients can be placed in a large bowl and mixed together with a spatula. So easy! Scoop out the dough with a tablespoon, roll it into a ball, place it on cookie sheet, and then flatten it slightly with your hand.

Bake for 12 to 15 minutes, rotating the cookie sheet about halfway through the baking time.

Yields 18 to 20 cookies.

COCONUTTY CHOCOLATE BROWNIE BARS

[BONNIE] You're going to love these brownie bars. We sometimes take a little help to make things easier and still have time to bake amid the whirlwind we call Life. This recipe starts with a gluten-free brownie mix. Several are available on the market, so discover your favorite—and then take it beyond decadent.

First Layer

    1 to 2 (20 oz.) box(es) gluten-free chocolate brownie mix

Second Layer

    2 (8 oz.) pkgs. cream cheese, room temperature

    ⅓ cup heavy cream

    6 T. powdered sugar

    1 tsp. vanilla

    3 cups Mounds Sweetened Coconut Flakes

Third Layer

    ⅓ cup heavy cream

    1 (12 oz.) pkg. dark chocolate chips

For the first layer, prepare the brownies according to the box instructions, bake, and cool.

For the second layer, mix the ingredients together and spread on top of layer one. Cover and refrigerate for 4 hours.

For the third layer, heat the heavy cream in the microwave until hot (about 2 minutes) and pour over the chocolate chips in a glass bowl. Mix until the chocolate is smooth and melted. Spread over second layer until it's completely covered.

Cover and chill for at least an hour. Then cut, serve, and enjoy.

Yields 10 to 12 servings.

NOTES

Not all brownie mixes are the same. Betty Crocker's, for instance, makes an 8 x 8-inch pan per box and Krusteaz's makes a 13 x 9-inch pan. That's why we said 1 to 2 boxes of brownie mix. We specified Mounds coconut because it is moist, sweet, and suggests the taste we're after. Feel free to use any brand you prefer, of course.

FRUIT JAM AND COCONUT BARS

[BONNIE] These taste a lot like the jam Christmas tarts we make but are so much quicker and easier to make. We usually prepare them with our favorite homemade strawberry or raspberry freezer jam. They both do well in this recipe, so choose whatever sounds good to you.

First Layer

1½ cups gluten-free 1-to-1 flour blend

½ cup (1 stick) butter, cubed and cold

1 egg

1 T. milk

Second Layer

1 cup strawberry or raspberry jam

Third Layer

4 T. (½ stick) butter, melted

¾ cup sugar

1 egg

1 cup sweetened flaked coconut

1 tsp. vanilla

Preheat the oven to 350°.

In a large bowl, combine the flour and ½ cup butter with a pastry cutter until it resembles coarse crumbs. Mix in the egg and milk. Pat the mixture in the bottom of a 13 x 9-inch pan and spread the jam over the first layer.

In another bowl, mix together the melted butter, sugar, egg, coconut, and vanilla. Carefully spread over the jam layer.

Place in the oven and bake for 30 minutes. Remove and allow to cool before cutting into bars.

Yields 12 to 16 bars.

HOMEMADE BROWNIES

[TAMI] Okay, confession time. I'd never made brownies completely from scratch before. With all of the great mixes out there, it was so simple to pick up a box of brownie mix, add a couple of ingredients, and be done. But since I decided to write a cookbook, it was time to try true homemade brownies. I rolled up my sleeves, ready for the arduous task, but it never came. Baking brownies from scratch was fun and almost as simple as using a mix. And the bonus? I knew exactly what I put into my bowl.

1 (4 oz.) pkg. Baker's unsweetened baking chocolate

¾ cup (1½ sticks) butter

2 cups sugar

1 cup gluten-free 1-to-1 flour blend

¼ tsp. salt

3 eggs

1 tsp. vanilla

1 cup nuts (optional)

1 cup chocolate chips (optional)

Preheat the oven to 325°. Grease a 13 x 9-inch baking dish and set aside. (You may use a smaller pan if you prefer. Keep in mind that the baking time will increase, but you will get thicker brownies.)

Break apart the baking chocolate into a microwave-safe bowl. Chunk up the butter and place it in the bowl as well. Microwave for 1 minute on high and stir. Return to the microwave and heat at 30 second intervals, stirring each time until the butter and chocolate are well blended. Stir in sugar.

Add the flour, salt, eggs, vanilla, and optional ingredients if you are using them. Pour the batter into a prepared pan and bake for 30 to 45 minutes or until a knife inserted into the middle comes out mostly clean (crumbs are okay, but you don't want wet dough on the knife).

Allow to cool completely before you cut apart and serve. If they are still warm, enjoy with a scoop of ice cream.

Yields 24 brownies.

LEMON RASPBERRY BARS

[BONNIE] This is a light, delicious summer dessert. It's quick and easy to prepare. You can make it early in the morning so you don't overheat your kitchen, and then it's chilled and ready later. We love lemon and raspberries, so this is a lovely combination of flavors. Because this recipe makes a small batch, you might need to make two pans.

Crust

6 T. butter

1½ cups gluten-free graham cracker crumbs

¼ cup C&H Baker's Sugar

Zest of 1 lemon

Filling

2 large egg yolks

1 (14 oz.) can sweetened condensed milk

½ cup fresh lemon juice

1 tsp. lemon zest

1 cup fresh raspberries

Preheat the oven to 350°.

In a microwave-safe bowl, melt the butter and then stir in the graham cracker crumbs, sugar, and lemon zest. Press into bottom of 8 x 8-inch pan. Bake for 10 minutes. Allow to cool.

While the crust is cooling, mix together the egg yolks, condensed milk, lemon juice, and zest. When all of that is thoroughly incorporated, carefully fold in the berries and then pour onto cool crust.

Place in the oven and bake for 15 minutes. Allow to cool and then cover and chill for at least one hour before serving.

Yields 9 bars.

NO-BAKE CHOCOLATE AND TOFFEE BARS

[BONNIE] How often do you wander into your kitchen hungry for something yummy, but you don't want to drag out a million dishes? This recipe may be a perfect option. And if you are like one of my sweet love bugs, you'll get your fix long before these bars are cooling in the refrigerator. "I help you, Bamma?" is shorthand for, "I'll stand beside you and stir every so often, dipping in with my adorable little fingers and tasting as we go!"

- 2¼ cups gluten-free graham cracker crumbs
- 1½ cups C&H Baker's Sugar, divided
- 1 cup (2 sticks) butter, divided
- 1 (12 oz.) pkg. chocolate chips
- 1 cup evaporated milk
- 1 (10 oz.) pkg. gluten-free miniature marshmallows (we use Kraft)
- 1 cup toffee bits
- 1 cup mini chocolate chips

Place the graham cracker crumbs and ½ cup of the sugar in a bowl. Melt ½ cup (1 stick) of the butter and pour over the graham cracker crumbs and sugar. Mix together and then press into the bottom of a 13 x 9-inch baking pan.

Place the chocolate chips from the bag into a large mixing bowl.

Combine the remaining sugar, butter, milk, and marshmallows in a saucepan and bring to a boil over medium heat. Continue to stir and watch carefully as you boil the mixture for 5 minutes. Remove from the heat and pour over the chocolate chips in the bowl. Whisk all of that together and then pour over the graham cracker crust. Sprinkle the top with the toffee bits and mini chocolate chips. Press them into the top slightly and then place in the refrigerator to chill for 2 hours.

Yields 12 to 24 bars.

NOTE

We realize not everyone loves toffee, and so we were brainstorming some options. You could add ½ cup peanut butter to the marshmallow mixture and then add peanut butter chips to the topping in place of the toffee bits. Or try using Reese's pieces or peanut butter M&M's. The sky… or the candy store…is the limit. I (Tami) tried this version for my husband's family reunion, and it was a hit. His aunt named this version "Chocolate Peanut Butter Fondue Bars."

NO-BAKE CHOCOLATE OATMEAL COOKIES

[BONNIE] These have been a family favorite since I was a little girl and a constant favorite when my children were growing up. We still make them for the grandchildren, but we have to make some with raisins and some without to make everyone happy.

2 cups C&H Baker's Sugar
½ cup (1 stick) butter
1 cup peanut butter
⅓ cup Hershey's baking cocoa powder
½ cup milk
1 tsp. vanilla
½ tsp. salt
3 cups gluten-free oatmeal
1 cup raisins (optional)

In a large saucepan mix together the sugar, butter, peanut butter, cocoa, and milk. Bring ingredients to boil over medium heat, stirring constantly to keep from burning, and allow to boil for 1 to 5 minutes until thickened.

Remove from the heat and stir in the vanilla, salt, and oats. Add the raisins if desired. Drop by spoonfuls onto cookie sheets covered with wax paper and refrigerate until firm.

Serves 8 to 12.

NOTE

Humidity and temperature have a lot to do with the thickening and hardening of this cookie. That is why I gave such a flexible cooking time. If a location is humid, candy can be temperamental, so it may take a little longer to thicken. Be attentive because the thickening process can go fast, and then you'll have a crumbly mess instead of yummy cookies.

NO-BAKE TOFFEE CHOCOLATE COOKIES

[BONNIE] Our two favorite flavors as a family are chocolate and caramel, so it goes without saying that we use them often. Here is another look at our old friends. We hope you love it!

½ cup (1 stick) butter

2 cups brown sugar

⅔ cup evaporated milk

½ tsp. sea salt

1 tsp. vanilla

3½ cups gluten-free oats

1½ cups toffee bits

1 cup mini chocolate chips

Place the butter, brown sugar, and milk in a large saucepan and stir over medium heat until the butter melts and all the ingredients are incorporated. Boil gently for 2 to 3 minutes, allowing the caramel to develop.

Remove from the heat and stir in the salt, vanilla, and oats. Allow to cool for 5 minutes. Stir in the toffee bits and place the dough by the spoonful onto cookie sheets lined with waxed paper. Carefully sprinkle the tops with the mini chocolate chips and then place the trays in the refrigerator to firm and chill.

Serves 8 to 12.

NO-FLOUR PEANUT BUTTER COOKIES

[BONNIE] At our house, we called these "magic peanut butter cookies" for years. This recipe came about when gluten-free was a new diagnosis and peanut butter cookies were in high demand. It was so awesome all those years ago to be able to make a cookie without flour. Gluten-free flour was scarce then, and what was available wasn't great. I hope you love these as much as we do.

1½ cups peanut butter

½ cup plus 2 T. C&H Baker's Sugar

½ cup brown sugar

1 egg, room temperature

1 tsp. vanilla

1 cup mini chocolate chips (optional)

Preheat the oven to 350°. Prepare a cookie sheet lined with parchment paper.

Cream the peanut butter and sugars together until light and fluffy. Add the egg and vanilla and mix well. Add the chocolate chips if using and chill the cookie dough for one hour. Then roll into 2-inch balls and place on the cookie sheet. Flatten the balls with the tines of a fork dipped in sugar.

Bake for 10 to 12 minutes.

Yields 2 to 4 dozen cookies.

PEANUT BUTTER CLOUDS

[BONNIE] These cookies fueled many car trips in the early years of our marriage. My husband and I were married in February, and that first summer we were on the road every single weekend except for two. We lived over a mountain pass from our families. My husband is also an avid sailor, so we were on the road attending racing events up and down the West Coast. I made these cookies fresh every Friday morning, did the laundry, packed the car, and, towing the boat, picked up my husband from work and we were off. To this day I can't eat one of these cookies without humming one of the old songs we used to sing along to on those trips—usually from one of our favorite musicals.

1 cup (2 sticks) butter, room temperature

1 cup peanut butter

1 cup brown sugar

2 cups powdered sugar

2 eggs, room temperature

1 tsp. vanilla

2 (250 grams) cups gluten-free 1-to-1 flour blend

2 tsp. baking soda

1 tsp. salt

A little sugar

Preheat the oven to 350°.

In a mixing bowl, cream together the butter, peanut butter, brown sugar, and powdered sugar until light and fluffy. Add the eggs one at a time and then vanilla until all is well combined.

In a separate bowl, combine flour, baking soda, and salt, whisking to break up any clumps. Slowly add to the wet mixture until everything is well incorporated. Remove the dough from the bowl and wrap in plastic wrap to chill in the refrigerator for half an hour.

Remove from refrigerator and form 1-inch balls, placing them down on baking sheets two inches apart. Using a fork dipped in sugar, press down the balls, making a crisscross pattern with the fork tines. Bake 12 to 15 minutes, remove from oven, and cool slightly.

Yields approximately 3 dozen cookies.

S'MORES COOKIE CUPS

[TAMI] Our family adores s'mores in any form, so these little handheld gems are a hit! We have several ways to change them up, but let's start with the basics and go from there.

> ½ cup (1 stick) butter
>
> 2 cups gluten-free graham cracker crumbs
>
> ½ cup sugar
>
> Miniature marshmallows
>
> Miniature chocolate chips
>
> Peanut butter cups (optional)
>
> Miniature candy bars (optional)
>
> Hershey's Kisses (optional)
>
> Marshmallow cream (optional)
>
> Toffee bits (optional)

Preheat the oven to 350°. Spray muffin pans with gluten-free, nonstick cooking spray.

Melt the butter in a microwaveable bowl and then stir in the graham cracker crumbs and sugar. Drop the crumb mixture into the muffin cups and press firmly into the bottom and up the sides. Place in the oven and cook for 5 minutes. Remove the pans and fill the crumb cups with miniature marshmallows and miniature chocolate chips and sprinkle with some of the loose graham cracker crumb mixture. Return to the oven for 2 to 3 minutes until the marshmallows brown.

Yields 1 dozen cookie cups.

NOTE

Instead of or in addition to miniature chocolate chips,
feel free to add any of the optional ingredients listed.
Same baking time applies, but all are delicious.

7

JUST DESSERTS

Sweetmeats of the Best Kind

Go, eat your food with gladness, and drink your wine with a joyful heart, for God has already approved what you do.

ECCLESIASTES 9:7

~

Apple Crisp

Butterfinger Caramel Cheesecake

Caramel Cream Cheese Frosting

Carrot Cake

Chocolate Chip Cheesecake

Chocolate Cream Pie

Chocolate Éclair Dessert

Chocolate Ganache

Chocolate Marshmallow Frosting

Chunky Applesauce Cake

Cream Cheese Frosting

Death-by-Chocolate Brownie-Crusted Chocolate Cheesecake

Dreamy Angel Food Cake

Fabulous Fruit Buckle

Fantastic Fudge Frosting

Fantastic Fudgy Chocolate Cake

Homemade Chocolate Cake

Old-Fashioned Vanilla Ice Cream

Old-Fashioned White Cake

Peanut Butter Ganache

Peanut Butter Jar Tarts

Powdered Sugar Frosting

Raspberry Sorbet

Salted Caramel Shortbread

Shirley Temple Cherry Cake

Strawberry Crisp

Strawberry Icebox Cake

Strawberry Poke Cake

Sweet Tooth Pound Cake

Triple Chocolate Cheesecake

Vanilla Pudding

~

[BONNIE] When we first moved to the community we live in now—nearly 30 years ago—we didn't know anyone. One of the ways we introduced ourselves was by baking treats and taking them to our closest neighbors. We'd moved into a neighborhood that was mostly comprised of retired folks, and our willingness to step out in friendship formed long-lasting bonds. Being open, vulnerable, and sharing sweets has grown into a holiday tradition. Some of our lovely neighbors have moved on, and new neighbors have taken their place, but our tradition continues.

This chapter is packed with old and new desserts sure to become passed-along treasures in your family too.

APPLE CRISP

[BONNIE] My mother used to make this recipe almost as often as any other dessert. Just the thought of apples and cinnamon makes me want to head to the kitchen.

Fruit Base

    10 to 12 large Granny Smith or Gravenstein apples,
        peeled, quartered, and sliced

    1 cup C&H Baker's Sugar

    2 tsp. cinnamon

Topping

    2 cups brown sugar

    1 tsp. cinnamon

    ½ cup (1 stick) butter, cold

    ¼ cup gluten-free 1-to-1 flour blend

Preheat the oven to 375°.

Combine the apples with the sugar and cinnamon in a large microwave-safe bowl. Cover with plastic wrap, cut a small hole to vent, and microwave for 10 minutes. Remove from microwave and place the apples in a large 13 x 9-inch baking dish.

In another bowl, combine the brown sugar and cinnamon, and then cut in butter until well combined. Add the flour and mix until crumbly. Cover the apples with the topping. Bake for 30 to 45 minutes until apples are done and topping is crunchy. Serve warm with a scoop of ice cream.

Serves 8 to 12.

BUTTERFINGER CARAMEL CHEESECAKE

[BONNIE] We never pass up an opportunity to make cheese-cake. Butterfinger candy bars and caramel… Yum! To think that about 20 years ago I made my first cheesecake to fulfill a birth-day request, and now we make them at the drop of a hat. We've grown more daring as the years have passed. That first one had mini chocolate chips with a regular crust—nothing fancy. Now…

Crust

2½ cups gluten-free graham cracker crumbs

½ cup Hershey's baking cocoa powder

½ cup C&H Baker's Sugar

½ cup (1 stick) butter, melted

Filling

4 (8 oz.) pkgs. cream cheese, room temperature

1 (14 oz.) can sweetened condensed milk

1⅓ cups C&H Baker's Sugar

1 tsp. vanilla

3 eggs

1 cup Butterfinger crumbles

Topping

½ cup Butterfinger crumbles

½ cup caramel dip

Preheat the oven to 350°. Wrap the bottom and sides of a springform pan in foil, making sure to overlap well so that no water can get in and make the crust soggy. Wrap the foil up to the top but not over the edge so it doesn't interfere with the top of the cheesecake as it bakes. Put the oven rack in the lower third of the oven.

In a mixing bowl combine the graham cracker crumbs, cocoa, and sugar. Stir well to combine. Stir in the melted butter until the crust is all combined. Pat firmly into the bottom of the prepared springform pan and bake for 10 minutes.

In the bowl of your stand mixer, or in a mixing bowl with a hand mixer, cream together cream cheese, condensed milk, and sugar until combined and smooth. Add the vanilla and the eggs one at a time until well combined, and then stir in Butterfinger crumbles by hand. Pour the filling into the crust. Place the springform pan in a large roasting pan and place in oven. Pour hot water into roasting pan, being careful not to splash cheesecake and only enough to reach about halfway up the side of the springform pan.

Reduce the heat to 300° and bake for 1 hour. Then turn off oven and, without opening the door, leave the cheesecake in the water bath for two hours. Remove, cover, and place in the refrigerator for at least four hours. When you are ready to serve, carefully remove the cheesecake from the springform pan and pour caramel over the top and then sprinkle with Butterfinger crumbles.

Serves 8 to 12.

NOTE

Graham crackers or prepared crumbs can be used (gluten-free, of course). And now a new item in the baking department is Butterfinger crumbles. You can also crunch up three or four candy bars if you can't find the ready-made crumbles. We also used store-bought caramel dip or caramel ice cream topping instead of making our own. As always, make sure you read the label carefully for gluten-free products.

CARAMEL CREAM CHEESE FROSTING

[BONNIE] This yummy frosting works well on any wonderful goodie you care to frost. If you love salted caramel, you can sprinkle some coarse sea salt on top.

1 cup (2 sticks) butter

4 oz. cream cheese

½ cup caramel dip

2 tsp. vanilla

4 cups powdered sugar

Cream together the butter and cream cheese in the bowl of stand mixer. When they are fluffy, add the caramel and vanilla. Increase the speed on mixer and whip on high. After 1 minute reduce the speed to low and carefully add the sugar a little at a time until all is combined. Return the speed to high and whip for 30 seconds and then reduce speed until the device is off. You're ready to frost!

Yields enough frosting to cover 2 to 3 layers of a round cake.

CARROT CAKE

[BONNIE] This cake was inspired by a cake made by one of our most-loved friends. Her cake was so moist and lovely that we had to come home and make our first-ever carrot cake! This dessert is so full of fruit, nuts, and carrots that you could maybe sneak it in as a meal if you close your eyes and pretend there is no thick, creamy cream cheese frosting!

2¾ cups brown sugar

½ cup C&H Baker's Sugar

1½ cups vegetable oil

4 eggs, room temperature

1 tsp. vanilla

2½ (312 grams) cups plus 1 T. gluten-free
    1-to-1 flour blend

2 tsp. cinnamon

1 tsp. baking soda

2 tsp. baking powder

½ tsp. salt

¼ tsp. cloves

½ tsp. nutmeg

Prepare 2 cake pans with gluten-free, nonstick cooking spray, line with parchment paper, and spray again.

In a bowl or mixer, cream together the sugars and oil, and then add the eggs one at a time to make sure they are well incorporated, and then add the vanilla.

In a separate bowl, combine the flour, cinnamon, baking soda, baking powder, salt, cloves, and nutmeg, mixing well with a whisk to make sure they are combined and that there are no lumps.

Slowly incorporate the dry ingredients into the creamed mixture until they are well combined. In the now-empty dry ingredients bowl, combine the raisins and pecans, sprinkle in the extra tablespoon of flour, and combine to make sure that the raisins and pecans are well coated so that they don't sink to the bottom of the cake. Set aside.

Stir the coconut, carrots, and pineapple into the cake batter and fold in the raisins and pecans last. Pour into the prepared pans and bake at 350° for 55 to 60 minutes or until golden brown and a toothpick comes out of the center nearly clean. Allow to cool completely and then frost with Cream Cheese Frosting or any one of your favorite frostings.

Yields two 9-inch round cake layers or one 13 x 9-inch cake.

CHOCOLATE CHIP CHEESECAKE

[BONNIE] Every year since she turned 13, my younger daughter asks for this cheesecake for her birthday because it's that good. Now that gluten-free graham crackers, and even graham cracker crumbs, are readily available in stores, it's easy to make this yummy dessert safe for her and the whole family.

Crust

    1 (8 oz.) box gluten-free graham crackers (or premade crumbs equaling 1 cup)

    3 T. C&H Baker's Sugar

    3 T. butter, melted

Filling

    3 (8 oz.) pkgs. cream cheese, room temperature

    ¾ cup C&H Baker's Sugar

    ½ cup heavy cream, room temperature

1 cup sour cream, room temperature

3 eggs, room temperature

1 cup mini chocolate chips

1 tsp. vanilla

Preheat the oven to 350°. Crush the graham crackers into fine crumbs or use premade crumbs. In a bowl, combine the graham cracker crumbs, sugar, and butter and then press the mixture into the bottom of a 9-inch springform pan. Bake for 10 minutes and allow to cool.

While the crust is baking, cream together the cream cheese and sugar, and then add the heavy cream and sour cream. Add the eggs one at a time. When the cream cheese mixture is thoroughly mixed, fold in chocolate chips and vanilla and then pour into the baked crust.

Bake the cheesecake in a water bath. Cover the springform pan with three overlapping sheets of heavy-duty foil, making sure no water will leak in to spoil crust. The foil should go all the way up the sides of the springform pan and can be scrunched together in such a way that the entire pan is covered but the foil doesn't spoil the top of the cheesecake as it rises.

Place the cheesecake in a large roasting pan big enough to hold it and fill the roasting pan with water until it comes halfway up the side of the springform pan. Place the roasting pan in lower third of the oven and bake at 325° for one hour.

Without opening the oven door, turn off the heat and leave the cheesecake in the oven without disturbing it for two more hours. At the end of that time, remove the cheesecake from the oven, leave the foil in place around the bottom, and then cover the top with plastic wrap, making sure it is covered completely so it doesn't dry out. Refrigerate for at least four hours or overnight before serving.

Serves 10 to 12.

CHOCOLATE CREAM PIE

[BONNIE] This recipe makes a wonderful, thick, chocolaty pudding that will make you forget about those boxed mix puddings that are not gluten-free. You can make different types of crust for this pie, so mix it up however your heart desires. My favorite part of cooking is when I can take a recipe and change it in a way that makes the dish personal. Experiment a little—just not on the day of an important party or event. (That last bit was personal experience talking.)

Crust

2¼ cups gluten-free chocolate graham cracker crumbs

½ cup (1 stick) butter, melted

½ cup C&H Baker's Sugar

Filling

1½ cups C&H Baker's Sugar

½ cup Hershey's baking cocoa powder

¼ cup cornstarch

¼ tsp. salt

3 cups half-and-half

4 egg yolks

6 oz. dark chocolate chips or chopped-up dark chocolate bars

2 tsp. vanilla

2 T. (¼ stick) butter

Preheat the oven to 375°.

In a small bowl, combine the graham cracker crumbs, butter, and sugar. Press into the bottom of a pie pan and bake for 10 minutes. Remove from the oven and allow to cool.

In a large saucepan, combine the sugar, cocoa, cornstarch, and salt, whisking to break up lumps and to thoroughly combine ingredients.

In a separate bowl, whisk together half-and-half and egg yolks, and then whisk them into the dry ingredients, mixing well.

Transfer to a saucepan and heat over low heat until the mixture reaches a simmer; cook for 10 minutes. Stir carefully, allowing the mixture to thicken and keep it from burning.

Place the chocolate chips or chunks in a bowl and then pour the hot mixture over them. Whisk to blend, and then add the vanilla and 2 T. butter. Mix well and pour into the crust. Carefully cover with plastic wrap, making sure the plastic wrap sits on top of the filling so that a skin doesn't form on the top, and place in the refrigerator, chilling for at least 2 hours before serving.

Serves 6 to 8.

CHOCOLATE ÉCLAIR DESSERT

[BONNIE] This dessert was passed down from a group of ladies, including my mother-in-law, whose husbands all worked together. All the couples and their families got together on camping trips multiple times each summer. They always potlucked the meals, so many fun dishes came back from these gatherings.

- 1 (5.9 oz.) box instant vanilla pudding
- 2 (3.9 oz.) boxes instant vanilla pudding
- 3 cups milk
- 1 (9 oz.) tub whipped topping
- 1 (7.5 oz.) box gluten-free graham crackers
- 1 (12 oz.) can of chocolate fudge frosting

In a large bowl, whisk together the vanilla pudding and milk. Allow to set for five minutes. Gently fold in the whipped topping.

Line the bottom of a 13 x 9-inch baking pan with graham crackers and cover with half of the pudding mixture. Cover with another layer of graham crackers and then cover with half of the frosting and the rest of the pudding. Finally, one more layer of crackers and the rest of the frosting. Cover and chill in the refrigerator until you are ready to eat.

Serves 9 to 12.

NOTE

Please make sure you read labels on the pudding mix, whipped topping, and frosting. We have favorites, but none of them are labeled gluten-free. We think Pamela's gluten-free graham crackers taste good. They are available online.

CHOCOLATE GANACHE

[BONNIE] Even though it sounds a bit like a highbrow, difficult glaze, if you follow these simple steps and don't rush it, this recipe might become the crown jewel in your repertoire. If you don't want to use it as a glaze, you can allow it to cool longer and make a delightful frosting or even truffles out of it.

1½ cups heavy cream

⅛ tsp. salt

1 (12 oz.) pkg. semi-sweet chocolate chips, chopped

Place the heavy cream and salt in a medium saucepan, and over medium heat bring the cream to a simmer and allow to simmer for 3 minutes. Remove from the heat and pour over the chocolate that you have placed in a glass bowl. Swirl the bowl to make sure that the chocolate is covered and then cover with a lid and allow to sit untouched for five minutes. Uncover and, using a whisk, start in the middle of the bowl and work outward until all the chocolate is glossy and smooth. Pour over the top of a cake or other dessert you wish to glaze. Allow to set up for as long as you can resist and then enjoy.

Yields 2 cups ganache.

NOTE

If you put the glaze in the refrigerator and allow it to cool completely, you can use a cookie scoop and roll it into balls to make lovely truffles.

CHOCOLATE MARSHMALLOW FROSTING

[TAMI] One of the amazing things about my mom is that she can pull together seemingly random ingredients and create something wonderful. During one birthday celebration, she was getting ready to frost the cake when the grandkids insisted marshmallows be a part of the frosting. Now this frosting has become one of my favorites and is a part of all my cakes, either as a filling or topping.

- 1 cup (2 sticks) butter, softened
- ½ cup + 1 T. unsweetened cocoa
- 2½ cups powdered sugar
- 1 T. vanilla
- 7 oz. marshmallow cream
- 2 to 4 T. milk, heavy cream, or sweetened condensed milk

Beat the butter until soft and fluffy. Add the remaining ingredients except for milk/cream/condensed milk and mix well. Add milk/cream/condensed milk until the desired consistency is achieved.

Yields frosting for one double-layer 10-inch round cake.

CHUNKY APPLESAUCE CAKE

[BONNIE] I loved how the house smelled when Mother was baking this applesauce cake. It was torture waiting for it to cool enough to frost. We always had our main meal on Sundays directly after church, and then we had this for our dessert after the evening service. We often invited friends back to the house, so desserts were extra special.

I like to make this now with homemade chunky applesauce because I love the occasional apple chunks that appear. We enjoy this dessert anytime, but it is a wonderful fall or Christmas cake.

½ cup (1 stick) butter, room temperature

2 cups C&H Baker's Sugar

2 eggs

1 tsp. vanilla

2½ cups (312.5 grams) gluten-free 1-to-1 flour blend

1½ tsp. baking soda

1 tsp. salt

1 tsp. cinnamon, ground

½ tsp. nutmeg, ground

½ tsp. allspice, ground

1½ cups Chunky Applesauce (see Chunky Applesauce in chapter 4)

½ cup raisins

½ cup chopped pecans

Preheat the oven to 350°. Spray the bottom and sides of a 13 x 9-inch baking pan with gluten-free, nonstick cooking spray.

In a large bowl, cream together butter and sugar until light and fluffy. Add the eggs one at a time, and then add the vanilla, mixing well.

In a separate bowl, combine the flour, baking soda, salt, and spices, using a small whisk to blend and make sure there are no clumps. Gradually add the flour mixture, and then the applesauce, to the creamed mixture until all is well combined. With a spatula, fold in raisins and pecans.

Pour the cake batter into baking pan and smooth the top. Bake for 45 minutes or until the cake is done in the center. Allow to cool and frost with buttercream or cream cheese frosting.

Serves 8 to 12.

CREAM CHEESE FROSTING

[BONNIE] This full-flavor frosting is a wonderful addition to carrot cake, cupcakes, and cookies. It can even be used on cinnamon rolls if maple frosting isn't your favorite. So many of the frostings and glazes in this cookbook can be used interchangeably on many desserts. You can recreate anything and make it your own by adding your own special touch. Have fun!

2 (8 oz.) pkgs. cream cheese, room temperature

½ cup (1 stick) butter, room temperature

4 cups powdered sugar

1 tsp. vanilla

½ tsp. salt

3 to 4 T. heavy cream

Cream together the cream cheese and butter, add the powdered sugar a ½ cup at a time, and then add the vanilla and salt. Add just enough heavy cream to bring the frosting to your preferred consistency. Frost your latest delicacy and enjoy.

Yields enough frosting for two 9-inch round cake layers or one 13 x 9-inch cake.

NOTE

Use regular cream cheese. It will make the frosting fluffier and better tasting than low- or zero-fat products do.

DEATH-BY-CHOCOLATE BROWNIE-CRUSTED CHOCOLATE CHEESECAKE

[BONNIE] We always let the birthday celebrant chose the dinner and cake. Tami said, "I want a chocolate cheesecake." Well, except for chocolate and cheesecake, that is totally up for interpretation, right? This is what I came up with, and fortunately it was a big hit! I was hoping the brownie layer would be more brownie-like having baked it first, but it all sort of melded together.

Try it, and you may find a new chocolate best recipe friend.

Brownie Crust

½ cup (1 stick) butter, room temperature

1 cup dark chocolate chips

1 cup (125 grams) gluten-free 1-to-1 flour blend

½ tsp. salt

1 cup C&H Baker's Sugar

1 tsp. baking soda

2 eggs, room temperature

¼ cup milk

1 tsp. vanilla

Cheesecake Layer

3 (8 oz.) pkgs. cream cheese, room temperature

¾ cup C&H Baker's Sugar

3 eggs, room temperature

1 tsp. vanilla

1 cup dark chocolate chips, melted

1 cup mini chocolate chips

Ganache

1½ cups heavy cream

2½ cups dark chocolate chips

Preheat the oven to 350° for the brownie layer. (After the brownies are baked, reduce the temperature to 325° for the cheesecake layer.) Wrap a 9-inch springform pan in three layers of heavy-duty aluminum foil and place a parchment paper round in the bottom of the pan. Spray with a gluten-free, nonstick cooking spray to keep the brownie layer from sticking to the pan.

Place the butter and dark chocolate chips in a microwave-safe bowl. Melt the chips by heating 30 seconds and stirring, heating and stirring, until the butter and chocolate are combined. Set aside.

In a larger mixing bowl, combine the flour, salt, sugar, and baking soda, whisking them to mix well.

In a smaller, bowl mix together the eggs, milk, and vanilla and then whisk into the dry ingredients. When combined, carefully whisk in the cooled melted chocolate and pour into the prepared springform pan. Place in the oven and bake for 30 minutes.

Meanwhile, place the cream cheese in a mixing bowl and cream with the sugar. Add the eggs one at a time, and then the vanilla. Stir in melted chocolate chips. When all is combined, carefully stir in the mini chips. Place the cheesecake mixture in refrigerator to keep chilled until the brownie layer is finished cooking and has cooled slightly.

When brownies are finished baking, move the oven shelf to the lower third of the oven. Reduce the heat to 325° and place the springform pan in a roasting pan that will hold enough very hot water to come halfway up the side. Place the springform pan in the water bath and pour the cheesecake mixture over the brownie layer and place it all back in the oven. Bake for 95 minutes. Turn off the heat, and without opening the oven door, allow the cheesecake to rest in the oven for one hour. At the end of the hour, remove it from the oven and then remove it from the springform pan. Place the cheesecake on a cake plate with a lip and place in the refrigerator to chill for four hours or overnight.

When the chilled cheesecake is ready, place the heavy cream in a microwave-safe bowl and heat for 1½ to 2 minutes. Place the dark chocolate chips in a heat-resistant bowl and pour the hot cream over them. Allow that chocolate and cream mixture to sit for 10 minutes, and then whisk the contents carefully together and pour over chilled cheesecake. Return to refrigerator until the ganache has set up and you are ready to serve. Chocolaty love or death, or both!

Serves 8 to 10.

DREAMY ANGEL FOOD CAKE

[BONNIE] As a child, this was one of my favorite cakes. It was often part of our Easter Sunday dinner. Although this recipe is gluten-free, you will swear it is not. And, if you follow the directions, it's nearly worry-free, and the result is so delicious you will wonder why you waited so long to try making an angel food cake from scratch.

¾ cup Bob's Red Mill Gluten-Free All-Purpose Baking Flour

¾ cup C&H Baker's Sugar

¼ cup cornstarch

1½ cups egg whites (10 to 11 large eggs)

¼ tsp. salt

1½ tsp. cream of tartar

2 tsp. vanilla extract

¼ tsp. almond extract

¾ cup plus 2 T. C&H Baker's Sugar

Preheat the oven to 350° and place a rack at the lowest setting.

Combine the flour, ¾ cup sugar, and cornstarch in a large bowl, running a whisk through it to mix the ingredients well and break up any clumps.

In the bowl of a stand mixer, or in a mixing bowl with a hand mixer, beat the egg whites, salt, and cream of tartar until foamy. Add the vanilla and almond extracts and continue beating, gradually increasing speed until the mixture is thickened and increased in volume. Gradually add in the ¾ cup plus 2 T. sugar until soft peaks form. Turn off the mixer and gently fold in the dry ingredients.

Carefully pour the batter into a 10-inch angel food cake pan (ungreased and completely clean and dry). Gently bang the bottom of the pan on the counter a couple of times to make sure that no big bubbles develop. Place the pan in the oven and bake for 45 minutes undisturbed or until golden brown.

Remove from the oven and suspend upside down on a glass bottle for two hours. Gently run a clean knife or spatula around the outside and neck of pan and place top down on a cake plate. Frost with a thick, creamy layer of buttercream frosting, or cut and serve with strawberries and a scoop of vanilla ice cream for a lovely strawberry shortcake.

Serves 8 to 12.

NOTE

I used Bob's Red Mill flour in this recipe, and it worked so nicely I didn't try any other flour. As always, we used C&H Baker's Sugar, and it worked perfectly.

FABULOUS FRUIT BUCKLE

[TAMI] This recipe came about after a day of blueberry picking. My daughter loves blueberries and thought it would be fun to try something new. This dessert is best served warm. For an extra-special treat, top with ice cream.

Buckle

2 cups gluten-free 1-to-1 flour blend

2½ tsp. baking powder

¼ tsp. salt

½ cup shortening

¾ cup sugar

1 egg, room temperature

½ cup milk, room temperature

2 cups blueberries or raspberries, fresh or frozen

Topping

½ cup gluten-free 1-to-1 flour blend

½ cup brown sugar

½ tsp. ground cinnamon

4 T. (½ stick) butter, cold

Preheat the oven to 350° degrees. Grease the bottom and sides of a 9 x 9-inch pan or an 8 x 8-inch pan.

In a medium bowl, combine the flour, baking powder, and salt.

In a medium mixing bowl, beat the shortening on medium speed for 30 seconds. Add the sugar and beat on medium speed until light and fluffy. Add the egg and continue to combine the ingredients well. Alternately add the flour mixture and milk, beating until smooth after each addition.

In another bowl, combine the flour, sugar, and cinnamon. Cut in the butter until the mixture resembles coarse crumbs.

Spoon the batter into the prepared pan. Sprinkle with the blueberries or raspberries and top with the topping. Bake for 50 to 60 minutes or until golden.

Serves 4 to 6.

NOTE

If you're keeping this to enjoy another day, store in an airtight container and warm up in the microwave.

I used Betty Crocker's 1-to-1 rice flour blend. This is a versatile recipe that should do well with other blends.

FANTASTIC FUDGE FROSTING

[BONNIE] When I was younger, we used to add chopped walnuts to this frosting and eat it as Christmas fudge. Since then, we've found easier ways to make fudge, but we still love this as frosting for Fantastic Fudgy Chocolate Cake.

    8 T. Hershey's baking cocoa powder

    3 cups C&H Baker's Sugar

    3 T. Karo light corn syrup

½ tsp. salt

1 cup evaporated milk

4 T. (½ stick) butter

1 tsp. vanilla

Butter the sides of a heavy-duty 3- to 4-quart saucepan. Combine the cocoa, sugar, corn syrup, and salt in the saucepan and then stir in milk. Cook over medium heat until sugar dissolves, stirring constantly. Avoid splashing the sides of the pan, stirring only to keep the mixture from sticking. The mixture should bubble gently over the entire surface. Continue cooking over medium heat until the soft ball stage (234°).

Remove from the heat and place the butter on top and allow to melt completely. Allow to cool to 110° without stirring. Add the vanilla and, using a sturdy spoon, beat the mixture in an up and over motion until frosting reaches spreading consistency, about 5 or 6 minutes.

Yields enough frosting to frost a two-layer round cake or a 13 x 9-inch sheet cake.

NOTE

Check the frosting's consistency often as you stir. It's surprising how long 5 minutes will seem. If you don't stir it long enough, it can be runny. Stir it too long, and it won't spread nicely.

FANTASTIC FUDGY CHOCOLATE CAKE

[BONNIE] This has been a family favorite since the Depression era. So much so that many of our family members ask for it to celebrate their birthday. It becomes even more of a star when it is frosted with Fantastic Fudge Frosting.

2 cups of gluten-free 1-to-1 flour blend

1 cup C&H Baker's Sugar

½ tsp. salt

8 T. Hershey's baking cocoa

1 tsp. baking soda

1 cup Best Foods mayonnaise (no substitutions)

1 cup water

2 tsp. vanilla

Preheat the oven to 350°. Spray the bottoms and sides of two cake pans with a gluten-free, nonstick cooking spray. Spray also the tops and bottoms of parchment rounds before placing them in the pans.

Combine the flour, sugar, salt, cocoa powder, and baking soda and mix well, using a whisk to blend and break up any lumps.

Mix together the mayonnaise, water, and vanilla and add slowly to the dry ingredients, mixing well.

Pour the batter in the cake pans and bake for 25 minutes or until a toothpick inserted in the center comes out clean. Allow to cool completely and frost with Fantastic Fudge Frosting (see our recipe in this chapter).

Yields a two-layer, 9-inch round cake.

HOMEMADE CHOCOLATE CAKE

[TAMI] I love chocolate cake. I eat it when I'm happy, sad, mad, or tired. I eat cake to celebrate or just because it's a Tuesday. I eat it here and there; I will eat it anywhere. (Apologies to Dr. Seuss.) I was so excited to discover that this cake tastes as good (or maybe better, you be the judge) as one made from a cake mix. Enjoy the freedom of being able to use everyday ingredients and not needing a boxed mix in your cupboard to enjoy cake…on a Tuesday!

2 cups (250 grams) gluten-free 1-to-1 flour blend

¾ cup unsweetened cocoa powder

1 tsp. baking soda

¾ tsp. baking powder

½ tsp. salt

¾ cup (1½ sticks) butter, softened

2 cups sugar

3 eggs, room temperature

2 tsp. vanilla

1½ cups milk

Preheat the oven to 350°. Grease two 9-inch round pans or two 8-inch square pans or one 13 x 9-inch baking dish.

In a medium bowl, combine the flour, cocoa powder, baking soda, baking powder, and salt and set aside.

In a large mixing bowl, beat the butter with an electric mixer until soft and fluffy. Add the sugar slowly, mixing as you go, and then beat on high for about 2 minutes. Scrape the sides of the bowl and then add the eggs and vanilla, beating for an additional 2 minutes on high.

Alternate adding the flour mixture and milk in small increments. Beat on a low speed between each addition to the batter until all of the flour and the milk are combined. Beat on high once again for approximately 1 minute.

Spread the batter into the prepared pan(s). Bake for 30 to 40 minutes or until a toothpick inserted into the middle comes out clean. Cool the cake completely before frosting or glazing. Chocolate Marshmallow Frosting is perfect for this cake—very decadent!

Serves 9 to 12.

OLD-FASHIONED VANILLA ICE CREAM

[BONNIE] Something we used to love most about family reunions in the summer is that there was always an ice cream freezer needing to be cranked. Now we use this same recipe in our electric ice cream freezer. It's still as delicious, but a little of the magic is gone. I miss my grandpa's chuckle when the ice cream got too thick for my little arms to push the crank through it. I miss my dad doing the same thing with my little chubby-cheeked babies. Now we have a new bunch of babies to make new memories with. God is so gracious—the circle of life continues.

    4 eggs
    2½ cups C&H Baker's Sugar
    8 cups half-and-half
    2 cups heavy whipping cream
    2½ T. vanilla
    ½ tsp. salt

Chill a 5-quart ice cream freezer.

Beat the eggs until a light yellow and then add the sugar gradually, beating until thick. Add the remaining ingredients and mix well. Pour into the ice cream freezer. Follow the directions for your device. (We always try to make it four hours or so before we want to eat it to allow the ice cream to become firm.)

Makes 16 to 20 servings.

OLD-FASHIONED WHITE CAKE

[BONNIE] This particular cake is so versatile it can be frosted, used as the backbone for a trifle, or as the beginning of a dump cake! Any way you use it, I hope it's part of a lovely celebration or an after-meal treat that makes someone feel loved or appreciated.

    2 cups gluten-free 1-to-1 flour blend
    1¼ cups C&H Baker's Sugar
    1 T. baking powder
    1 tsp. salt
    ½ cup (1 stick) butter, room temperature
    1 cup milk
    1 tsp. vanilla
    2 eggs, room temperature

Preheat the oven to 350°. Prepare either a 13 x 9-inch pan or two 8-inch round pans by using gluten-free, nonstick cooking spray and then parchment paper cut to the fit the pan and sprayed with the cooking spray again.

In a large bowl, combine the flour, sugar, baking powder, and salt and whisk together until well incorporated. Add the butter, milk, and vanilla, mixing well, and continue to whip for 2 minutes.

Add the eggs one at a time and continue to whip for 2 additional minutes. When all is fluffy and combined, pour the batter in the prepared pan(s). Bake for 30 to 35 minutes or until golden brown and toothpick comes out of the center clean.

Yields one 13 x 9-inch cake or two 8-inch round cakes.

PEANUT BUTTER GANACHE

[BONNIE] This is another glaze you can use on a chocolate cake, cupcakes, or cookies. Or, as with the Chocolate Ganache, allow it to cool completely and create lovely truffles.

    10 oz. dark chocolate chips or fine chocolate, chopped
    ½ cup creamy peanut butter
    1½ tsp. vanilla
    1½ cups heavy cream

Place the chocolate, peanut butter, and vanilla in a glass bowl and set aside. Place the heavy cream in a saucepan and over medium heat bring to a simmer and allow to simmer for 3 minutes.

Remove from the heat and pour the cream over the chocolate and peanut butter and cover with a lid. Allow to sit for ten minutes. Remove lid and, using a whisk, start in the middle of bowl and work outward, whisking until ganache is shiny and smooth. Allow to cool slightly and then pour over a cake or other delicacy.

Yields 2 cups ganache.

NOTE

If you wish to make the ganache into truffles, cover with plastic wrap and place in refrigerator until completely chilled. Using a cookie scoop, make small balls and then cover with chocolate ganache or powdered sugar, and you have delicious truffles.

PEANUT BUTTER JAR TARTS

[BONNIE] This is a fun, easy recipe that provides a delightful way to serve dessert for holiday parties or showers, or is just an easy way to portion desserts for lunches. The popularity of canning jars now makes this a great way to serve this scrumptious sweet treat.

1 cup powdered sugar

1 (8 oz.) pkg. cream cheese, room temperature

1 cup creamy peanut butter

1 (16 oz.) container whipped topping, thawed, divided

1½ cups gluten-free graham cracker crumbs

1½ cups mini chocolate chips

Wash and dry 12 (1 pint) canning jars and lids.

Cream together the powdered sugar, cream cheese, and peanut butter. When they are well combined and fluffy, carefully fold in ½ the whipped topping.

Place a tablespoon of graham cracker crumbs in the bottoms of all the jars. Cover the crumbs with the mini chocolate chips and then spoon a layer of the peanut butter filling over the chocolate. Layer a spoonful of whipped topping in each and then repeat layers. Continue to layer until you run out of ingredients, ending with whipped topping sprinkled with a few chocolate chips and perhaps even some of the cracker crumbs. Screw on the lids and place the desserts in the refrigerator until you're ready to serve.

Serves 12.

POWDERED SUGAR FROSTING

[BONNIE] This frosting was always our go-to treat topper when I was a child, and it still is today. We use it when we make Christmas cookies and all kinds of cake, and we even use it to frost graham crackers. According to my grandchildren, nearly everything is better with frosting.

½ cup (1 stick) butter, room temperature

1¾ lbs. powdered sugar

¼ cup evaporated milk or light cream

2 tsp. vanilla

Cream together the butter and powdered sugar. Gradually add milk or cream (only enough to make spreading consistency) and the vanilla. Frost your baked goodies and enjoy.

Yields frosting for one 13 x 9-inch cake.

RASPBERRY SORBET

[BONNIE] The other day we were visiting a favorite local farm, and they had the loveliest raspberries. I bought an entire flat intending to make jam. But I decided halfway through to try some sorbet since it is a particular favorite of my husband. He loved it! I hope you do too. The good news is this recipe can translate to your favorite flavor for a tasty treat any time of year.

6 pints fresh raspberries, cleaned and pureed

1 cup C&H Baker's Sugar

1 cup water

1 to 4 T. fresh lemon juice

Freeze the tub of your ice cream maker 24 hours before you plan to make the sorbet.

Run the pureed raspberries through a superfine mesh strainer to remove the seeds. (Be careful not to force the berries through the mesh with too much force so as not to force the seeds through.) Set aside.

In a small saucepan, combine the water and sugar over medium-low heat and stir until all of the sugar is dissolved. Simmer for approximately 5 minutes and allow to cool.

Mix a ½ cup of this simple syrup into the berries and then stir in 1 T. of the lemon juice. Taste and add additional lemon juice as desired. Cover and chill until you are ready to process.

Following the directions for your ice cream maker, place the pureed fruit in the tub and process for at least 15 minutes. When thickened, resembling a very thick smoothie, remove from the tub and pour into plastic freezer containers and freeze until ready to enjoy.

Serves 6 to 8.

SALTED CARAMEL SHORTBREAD

[BONNIE] Talk about a crowd-pleaser! People love this simple dessert. Even better, they're shocked to find out it is gluten-free. Instead of caramel apple dip, you could also make the caramel from scratch or unwrap 50 baking caramels and melt them over low heat with milk or cream. We like the dip for ease—and it tastes just as good.

Crust
2½ cups (5 sticks) butter, room temperature

1½ cups C&H Baker's Sugar

2¼ cups powdered sugar

3 T. vanilla

6 cups (750 grams) gluten-free 1-to-1 flour blend

Filling
1 (16 oz.) container caramel apple dip

1 T. coarse sea salt

Preheat the oven to 350°. Line a cookie sheet with foil or parchment paper.

Combine the butter, sugars, and vanilla, and then add the flour. Mix in a cup at a time. Once combined, press half the dough into the bottom of the cookie sheet. Place the remaining dough in the refrigerator. Bake the crust for 20 minutes or until pale brown. Let cool for 15 minutes.

Spread the caramel dip on top of the cooled crust and sprinkle with salt. Crumble the remaining dough on top of the caramel layer. Bake 25 to 30 minutes or until golden brown. Remove from oven and allow to cool before cutting into bars.

Serves 18 to 24.

NOTE

The first time we made this recipe, we used a gluten-free baking mix, and it came out a little difficult to cut. Now we make it with a good 1-to-1 flour blend, which means it's formulated for baking to be an equal substitute to 1 cup of wheat flour. We like Bob's Red Mill products, but make sure you check the labels.

SHIRLEY TEMPLE CHERRY CAKE

[BONNIE] Shirley Temple stole my heart when I was young. I wanted to be her! Apparently, the first of her movies I ever saw was one Thanksgiving when I was three years old. It was her version of *Heidi*. We were at my grandparents' watching it on TV. I was so caught up in the story that when the "Alm Uncle" chased Heidi and her aunt down the mountain into the village, my parents found me cowering behind my grandfather's chair. That scene has stayed with me to this day. Here's a cake to go with my Shirley Temple memories.

3 cups gluten-free 1-to-1 flour blend

2½ tsp. baking powder

1 tsp. salt

1½ cups sugar

⅓ cup shortening

⅓ cup (½ stick plus 1 T.) butter, room temperature

¼ cup maraschino cherry juice

¾ cup milk

1 tsp. almond extract

16 maraschino cherries, cut in eighths

5 egg whites, stiffly beaten

Preheat the oven to 350°. Prepare a 13 x 9-inch baking pan or two 8-inch cake pans by spraying them with gluten-free, nonstick cooking spray.

In a large bowl, combine the flour, baking powder, and salt. Whisk together until well combined. Set aside.

In a mixing bowl, cream together the sugar, shortening, and butter. Place the cherry juice, milk, and almond extract into a measuring cup. Alternating between the liquid and the dry ingredients, add ⅓ of each to the creamed mixture, mixing well. Repeat two more times.

Stir the cherry pieces into the batter and then set aside while you whip the egg whites in a separate bowl. When they are whipped to stiff peaks, carefully fold them into the batter and then pour into the prepared pan(s).

Bake for 30 to 35 minutes or until golden brown and a toothpick inserted into the center comes out clean. Remove from oven and allow to cool completely. Frost with any of the frostings you can find in this cookbook. (You could add more of the cherry juice to one of the white frostings to make it pink and use the rest of the cherries to decorate the cake.)

Yields one 13 x 9-inch or two 8-inch round cakes.

NOTE

You can overbeat egg whites. One time I became so involved with something while the egg whites were

in the mixer whipping away that when I came back,
they looked a little like sea foam after a hard winter
storm—a big mass of foam that was nearly brick-like.

STRAWBERRY CRISP

[BONNIE] Have you ever gone to a local farm stand, come home with a flat of berries, and then realized the berries are ripe NOW and you can't get to the store for the ingredients you are lacking? That's where this recipe came from.

6 cups strawberries, washed, hulled, halved

½ cup C&H Baker's Sugar

2 T. cornstarch

2 cups gluten-free 1-to-1 flour blend

1½ cups gluten-free graham cracker crumbs

1 cup brown sugar

1 tsp. baking powder

1 tsp. salt

1 cup (2 sticks) butter, cold

Preheat the oven to 375°.

Place the strawberries in a bowl and then add the sugar and cornstarch. Set aside.

In a large mixing bowl, combine the remaining dry ingredients and mix well, using a whisk to break up any lumps. Cut in the cold butter with a pastry cutter until the mixture resembles pea-sized crumbs.

Press half of the mixture in the bottom of a 13 x 9-inch baking dish and bake for 10 minutes. Remove from the oven and carefully spoon the berries and juice over the bottom crust. Cover with the remaining crumb mixture. Return the pan to oven and bake until browned, approximately 25 minutes.

Serves 8 to 12.

STRAWBERRY ICEBOX CAKE

[BONNIE] This old-fashioned dessert is easy, yummy, and the perfect treat during the long days of summer. It takes just minutes to put together, and you don't have to heat up the kitchen. You'll be the heroine of the heat wave!

    5 cups heavy whipping cream
    1 tsp. vanilla
    1 cup C&H Baker's Sugar
    12 gluten-free graham crackers
    3 cups fresh strawberries, washed, hulled, and sliced

Whip the whipping cream, vanilla, and sugar together until stiff peaks form.

In the bottom of a 9 x 9-inch pan, paint a layer of whipped cream and then place a layer of the graham crackers, a layer of whipped cream, a layer of strawberries, whipped cream, crackers, and so on. Repeat the layers until your ingredients run out, making sure that you end with strawberries on top. Cover the pan with plastic wrap and place it in the refrigerator for three hours.

Serves 8 to 10.

STRAWBERRY POKE CAKE

[TAMI] I've been blessed in that once I was diagnosed, not only did my side of the family help come up with dishes and things for me to eat, but my mother-in-law did as well. In fact, she and my mother started digging through old family recipes and trying new flours and mixes to make the concoction resemble the gluten-containing version they knew so well. This is one of those recipes my mother-in-law created for me.

    1 yellow or white gluten-free cake mix, and required
       ingredients listed in box directions
    1 (6 oz.) pkg. strawberry Jell-O
    2 cups water, boiling

1 (16 oz.) pkg. frozen strawberries, thawed

1 (16 oz.) carton whipped topping, thawed

10 fresh strawberries, halved, with leaves removed

Other fresh berries (optional)

Preheat the oven according to the cake mix directions. Grease a 13 x 9-inch baking dish.

Prepare and bake the cake mix in the 13 x 9-inch baking dish. Once the cake comes out of the oven, combine the Jell-O and boiling water until well mixed. Stir in the thawed strawberries.

With a sharp knife, score the top of the cake with an *X* and poke a few holes as well. Pour the Jell-O and strawberries over the cake. Let the cake cool completely before placing in the refrigerator for at least 6 hours. Spread whipped topping over the cake and garnish with strawberries or other fresh berries as desired.

Serves 8 to 12.

NOTE

We've used this cake for Easter, Fourth of July, birthday celebrations, and potluck gatherings. Using different fresh berries on top as decorations to match the theme adds variety and fun.

~

Here's our low-sugar option:

Use ¼ cup unsweetened applesauce, 2 egg whites, 1 egg, and 1⅓ cups water in place of the added ingredients listed on the cake mix package. Mix on low speed for 30 seconds, and then on high for 2 minutes. Bake at 350° for 20 to 35 minutes or until a toothpick comes out clean. Follow the directions above, replacing the Strawberry Jell-O with Sugar-Free Strawberry Jell-O and the whipped topping with a reduced-fat whipped topping.

SWEET TOOTH POUND CAKE

[TAMI] This is a tender, crumbly, sweet pound cake. A perfect pairing for all the delicious berries available in the summer. We love pound cake—lemon, chocolate, and this one, also a star.

1¼ cups (2½ sticks) butter, room temperature

2½ cups C&H Baker's Sugar

1 (14 oz.) can sweetened condensed milk

2 tsp. vanilla

6 eggs

3½ cups 1-to-1 gluten-free flour blend

1½ tsp. baking powder

½ tsp. salt

Spray two large bread pans with gluten-free, nonstick cooking spray and line with parchment paper.

Place the butter and sugar in the bowl of a stand mixer and mix on low until light and fluffy. While still mixing, add the condensed milk and vanilla and completely incorporate. Then add one egg at a time, waiting until each one is mixed in before adding the next one.

In a separate bowl combine the flour, baking powder, and salt and whisk together to make sure they are combined and all clumps are gone. Carefully add the dry ingredients to the wet a little at a time until everything is completely combined.

Pour the batter in the prepared bread pans. (If your pans aren't large enough to hold all the batter, use whatever else you have that will hold the batter and prepare it the same way as your bread pans.) Place the pans in oven and bake at 350° for at least 1 hour. Then check with a toothpick. If not quite done, increase the baking time in 10-minute increments until a toothpick comes out clean.

Remove from the oven and cool in the pans for at least 30 minutes. Remove from the pans, slice generously, and slather with your favorite fruit. Or you can frost with our Caramel Cream Cheese Frosting and serve with sliced peaches. Mmm, good!

Serves 6 to 12.

NOTE

We tried this recipe in a Bundt pan, but in gluten-free baking
you need to line the pans. Let me tell you, it was not pretty!

TRIPLE CHOCOLATE CHEESECAKE

[TAMI] If you love chocolate, this is a to-die-for treat. To. Die.
For. Cheesecake and chocolate are both family favorites, so this
dessert is a winner on all counts. You won't be disappointed.

Crust

1 cup gluten-free chocolate graham cracker crumbs

3 T. C&H Baker's Sugar

3 T. butter, melted

Cheesecake Filling

3 cups mini chocolate chips, divided

3 (8 oz.) pkgs. cream cheese, room temperature

1 (14 oz.) can sweetened condensed milk

4 eggs, room temperature

2 tsp. vanilla

Chocolate sundae syrup (garnish)

In a medium-sized bowl, mix together the graham cracker
crumbs, sugar, and butter. Press into the bottom of 9-inch
springform pan.

Melt 2 cups of the chocolate chips in microwave-safe bowl,
stirring at 30 second intervals until smooth and melted.

In a large bowl, beat the cream cheese until fluffy, gradually adding
the condensed milk until smooth. Add the melted chocolate,
the eggs one at a time, and the vanilla. Fold in the remaining
chocolate chips and pour the batter into the springform pan.
Overlap three sheets of heavy-duty foil, making sure no cracks will
let in water, crimping the tops together so that the rim of the pan

is covered but the top of the cake will not be disturbed. Place the springform pan in a large roasting pan and add enough hot water to go halfway up the side of springform pan.

Place in the bottom third of the oven and bake at 300° for 65 minutes. Turn off the heat but do not disturb for 2 hours.

Remove from the oven, cover, and refrigerate for 4 hours or overnight. When you're ready to serve, drizzle with chocolate syrup.

Serves 10 to 12.

VANILLA PUDDING

[BONNIE] Just like the velvety chocolate pudding used in the Chocolate Cream Pie, this recipe should help if you are craving a creamy vanilla treat. It can be used in pie, pudding cups, trifles, and layered desserts. Best of all, also as an after-nap treat for your little love bugs! (Sorry. The grandma in me just popped out again. But remember, what happens at Grandma's house stays at Grandma's house.)

⅔ cup C&H Baker's Sugar
¼ cup cornstarch
¼ tsp. salt
2⅔ cups half-and-half
4 large egg yolks
4 tsp. vanilla
2 T. (¼ stick) butter

In a large saucepan, whisk together the sugar, cornstarch, and salt.

In a separate bowl, whisk together the half-and-half and egg yolks, and then whisk them into the dry ingredients in the saucepan. Over low heat, bring the mixture to a simmer and allow to simmer for 10 minutes. When thickened, remove from the heat and add the vanilla and butter, combining completely. Pour the pudding into individual bowls, cover the top of the pudding with plastic wrap to keep it from forming a skin, and chill for two hours.

Yields about 3 cups pudding.

8

HOLIDAYS

Let Them Be Jolly

*Blessed is she who has believed that the
Lord would fulfill his promises to her!*

LUKE 1:45

~

Christmas Colors Salad

Christmas Tarts

Cranberry Apple Cider Punch

Cranberry Fruit Dip

Decadent Mashed Potatoes

Dublin Cabbage Coddle (Stew)

Emperor's Dressing

Family Favorite Fudge

Festive Holiday Ham

God Bless America Fruit Salad

Holiday Gravy

Independence Day S'mores Bars

Lucky Irish Soda Bread

Pecan Pie Bars

Pumpkin Cake

Pumpkin Cheesecake Bars

Red, White, and Blue
Cheesecake Nibbles

Snow-Topped Chocolate
Mint Cookies

Spiced Apple Cider

Succulent Turkey

Twice-Baked Sweet Potatoes

~

[BONNIE] I love Luke 1:45. Yes, it's about Mary, but it can also be about us. I remember the first women's Bible study Christmas celebration I went to as a new bride. We sipped mulled cider and exchanged white elephant gifts, and then we stood around the lit tree and began to worship. As we sang "Silent Night," a young mother who had a brand-new little boy in her arms was rocking him quietly when he started to whimper a little. It was so precious that we all had tears flowing down our cheeks when we finished. Such a perfect gift from God. No one spoke. We just hugged one another and filed out the door into a cold, starlit night, certain that we had been in God's presence.

Holidays are a big deal in our family. We make sure that worship, prayer, and praise are a significant part of our celebration. Of course, another important aspect is the food. We hope you find something in our traditions that you can make your own, and that your celebrations are filled with love, family, and joy.

CHRISTMAS COLORS SALAD

[BONNIE] The colors in this salad make me feel happy because the holidays are my absolute favorite time of the year. For every gathering we like to start with a theme and decorate the house, the table, and even the food to create the ambience. This is a simple salad yet so fun when at the center of a holiday table.

Salad

  2 cups cauliflower florets

  2 cups broccoli florets

  2 cups grape tomatoes, halved

  ½ red onion, thinly sliced

  1 (3.8 oz.) can sliced black olives

  2 cups fresh, small mozzarella balls (cut in half or smaller depending on the size)

Dressing

  3 T. extra virgin olive oil

  2 T. parsley, finely chopped

  1 T. apple cider vinegar

  ½ tsp. garlic salt

  ⅛ tsp. pepper

Place all of the vegetables in a large salad bowl and add the cheese. In a small bowl, whisk the dressing ingredients together and pour over the salad. Cover and refrigerate at least two hours or longer until time to serve.

Serves 8 to 12.

CHRISTMAS TARTS

[TAMI] All the women in Grandma Root's extended family gathered when she was young and had a marathon tart-making day every year just before Christmas. She looked forward to it every year. So much so, that even when she grew up and moved away, she still made them for her family. It's a treat still cherished and anticipated by the whole family.

Shell

> ¾ cup (1½ sticks) butter
>
> ⅓ cup shortening
>
> ½ cup water
>
> 3 cups gluten-free 1-to-1 flour blend
>
> 1 tsp. salt
>
> 1 T. C&H Baker's Sugar

Filling

> Strawberry or raspberry jam

Topping

> ¼ cup (½ stick) butter
>
> 1 cup sugar
>
> 2 eggs, well beaten
>
> 1 cup white rice flour

Preheat the oven to 350° degrees.

Dice the ¾ cup butter into small cubes and put it and shortening in freezer to chill. Measure the water and add ice cubes to keep it cold.

In a large bowl, combine the flour, salt, and sugar and mix well. When the butter and shortening are very cold, cut them into the flour mixture until pea-sized crumbs develop. Discard the ice, and gradually add only enough water to bring the dough together.

Divide the dough into fourths and place one-fourth on a floured board (use additional 1-to-1 gluten-free flour). Place the other three parts of the dough in the refrigerator to keep cold. Using a rolling pin, roll out the dough until it's about ⅛ inch thick. Cut out circles that will fit in your tart pans. (We use mini muffin tins, but use whatever you have.)

To make the topping, melt the butter in a small saucepan, remove from the heat, and stir in the sugar. In a small bowl, slightly whisk the eggs and rice flour together until there are no lumps and then whisk in butter mixture until well combined. Set aside.

Fill the tart shells with a ½ tsp. of jam and top with a ½ tsp. of topping. Bake for 20 minutes or until the crust and topping are golden brown.

Yields 12 to 24 tarts.

NOTE

We line the bottom of the muffin cups with parchment to help get the tarts to release cleanly. It takes some time to measure and cut the parchment, but it will be worth it to have nice-looking tarts.

CRANBERRY APPLE CIDER PUNCH

[BONNIE] This punch is so pretty and refreshing. With so many reasons to get together and celebrate in the fall and winter, you can never have too many special recipes for flavorful drinks. I love it when the food and drink not only look and taste great, but also add to the ambience.

1 cup fresh cranberries

⅓ cup water

½ cup sugar

4 cups apple cider

2 T. fresh lemon juice

2 cups cranberry juice

2 cups ginger ale

In a small sauce pan, combine the cranberries and water and simmer for 2 to 3 minutes until the cranberries start to pop.

Remove from the heat, stir in the sugar, and allow to cool to room temperature. Place in a large pitcher and refrigerate. When completely chilled, add the rest of the ingredients except for the ginger ale and refrigerate until ready to serve.

When ready to serve, add the ginger ale and then pour over glasses filled with ice.

Serves 4 to 8.

CRANBERRY FRUIT DIP

[TAMI] This is a fruit dip my sister-in-law came up with that I have since used for many potluck events and family gatherings. This is a great dish for sharing that promotes fellowship—it will keep them coming back for more. With only three ingredients and a 5-minute prep time, this dish is easy to throw together on your way out the door.

4 oz. cream cheese, softened

1 cup whole berry cranberry sauce

1 cup whipped topping, thawed

Beat the cream cheese until softened. Add the cranberry sauce and mix together until well combined. Gently fold in the whipped topping and serve.

Serves 6 to 10.

NOTE

This dip is great served with fresh fruit, Chewy Gingersnaps (see our recipe in chapter 6), or graham crackers. Also, you can just pull out a spoon!

DECADENT MASHED POTATOES

[BONNIE] As a child, if there wasn't meat, potatoes, and bread on the table, it wasn't dinner, so mashed potatoes was one of the first things I learned to make. From a young age I thought peeling potatoes was boring, so now I don't peel them, and we actually enjoy the taste even more. These are so decadent, they are the perfect special treat for the holidays.

    1 (5 lb.) bag baby golden or red potatoes, halved
    1 to 2 tsp. salt
    1½ cups sour cream
    1 cup (2 sticks) butter
    1 cup cheddar cheese, shredded (optional)
    1 (8 oz.) pkg. cream cheese (optional)

Place the potatoes in a large saucepan, covering them completely with water, and add the salt. Bring to a boil and cook until fork tender, approximately 20 minutes.

Remove the pan from the stove and drain off the water. Add the sour cream, butter, and any optional ingredients. Using a hand mixer, whip everything together until all of the lumps are gone and the ingredients are completely incorporated. Serve with or without gravy or additional butter. They are that good!

Serves 4 to 6.

DUBLIN CABBAGE CODDLE (STEW)

[BONNIE] Does your family have favorites you make for certain holidays? This was always our dinner for Saint Patrick's Day. I thought it was an authentic meal, but it turns out it was adapted from several dishes and became our own version. All the Dublin Coddles I've seen recipes for don't have cabbage. Most cabbage dishes have bacon and no sausage. But after reading all those recipes, ours has both now. The good news is, most children don't really care if dishes are authentic. All they care about are the fun, memory making moments.

8 slices bacon, thickly sliced

1 lb. high-quality pork sausage (bangers, bratwurst, or even Polish sausage)

1 onion, sliced

2 lbs. baby red potatoes, cut in ½-inch cubes

1 large green cabbage

3½ cups chicken broth

Salt and pepper to taste

In a large Dutch oven, brown the bacon until it starts to crisp. Remove from the pan and drain on paper towels. Reserve most of the bacon fat. In the same pan, cook the sausages until they are evenly browned and then remove them from the pan and set aside.

Add back 1 T. of the bacon fat and cook the onion slices for 2 to 3 minutes. Remove from the heat and cut the bacon into fourths. The sausages should be cut in halves or smaller, depending on the size of the sausages.

Layer the bacon, onion, and sausages in the bottom of the pan. Add the potatoes and then place the cabbage on top after you have cut the head in half, removed the core, and then cut it into halves again. Cover with broth and bring the entire pot to boil. Cook until the potatoes are fork tender.

We used to drain and serve with a pat of butter, salt, and pepper, but you could just as easily serve with the broth and eat as a hearty stew.

Serves 6.

EMPEROR'S DRESSING

[BONNIE] Even with the tongue-in-cheek name, this yummy dressing is no joke. This is the dressing we used to have at every Thanksgiving and Christmas dinner as a child. It's a great side dish that can be eaten alone or with gravy. Honestly, I had family members who loved gravy or jam so much…well, that's another story.

- ¼ cup (½ stick) butter
- ½ cup onion, diced
- ½ cup celery, diced
- ½ cup mushroom caps, diced
- 4 cups gluten-free bread cubes, cut up and baked until dry and crisp
- 1 to 2 cups chicken broth
- 1 tsp. poultry seasoning
- 1 tsp. sage
- Salt and pepper to taste

Preheat the oven to 325°.

In a large skillet, melt the butter and add the diced vegetables, sautéing until they are softened. Place the bread cubes and vegetables in a large bowl. Pour just enough broth over the top to moisten, add seasonings, and then stir all of the ingredients together until combined. Place the mixture in a 2-quart oven-safe casserole dish, cover, and bake for 30 minutes. If you are roasting a turkey, it can be baked alongside the turkey in its final 30 minutes of roasting time.

Serves 8.

NOTE

If you are also preparing Holiday Gravy for your meal, and you choose not to add the giblets to that gravy, you could add them to the bowl with the bread crumbs and sautéed vegetables when making this dressing.

FAMILY FAVORITE FUDGE

[BONNIE] This is a recipe that came from my mother-in-law as a family favorite long before I got married. Over the years, I've changed ingredients as needed until we came to this version. We share it with family, neighbors, and friends. Making fudge has become a much-anticipated Christmas tradition. Perhaps it can become one of yours.

> 6 (12 oz.) pkgs. dark chocolate chips
>
> 2 tsp. vanilla
>
> ½ tsp. salt
>
> 1 (14 oz.) jar marshmallow cream
>
> 6 cups C&H Baker's Sugar
>
> 2 (12 oz.) cans evaporated milk
>
> 2 cups (4 sticks) butter

Spray 6 tin pie pans with gluten-free, nonstick cooking spray. Place the chocolate chips, vanilla, salt, and marshmallow cream in a large bowl.

In a large Dutch oven over medium heat, combine the sugar, evaporated milk, and butter, stirring constantly until the mixture comes to a boil. Continue to cook for 4 more minutes or until a candy thermometer reads 235°.

Remove from the heat and stir into the bowl with the chocolate chips and marshmallow cream, working fast so the chocolate doesn't seize. When smooth and incorporated, pour into the pie pans. Spread out to cover the bottoms of all the pans and smooth the tops. Cover with foil and refrigerate until firm.

When the time comes to share, cut into small squares and place on a festive serving plate. As the fudge warms, it becomes less firm, so we never cut too much at once.

Yields 6 trays of fudge.

FESTIVE HOLIDAY HAM

[TAMI] This ham has long been a family favorite for holidays and other special gatherings. We love it as part of Christmas or Easter dinner, but it's also so yummy in sandwiches, omelets, or even soup as leftovers.

> 3- to 5-lb. ham
> Whole cloves
> 1 (20 oz.) can pineapple rings (packed in own juice)
> ⅛ cup (¼ stick) butter, melted
> Brown sugar

Place the ham in a slow cooker, score the top with a sharp knife, and then dot with whole cloves, taking advantage of the score marks. Arrange pineapple rings on top of ham, using the cloves to help hold pineapple in place.

Pour the juice and melted butter into a large measuring cup, adding enough brown sugar to make a thick syrup. Pour the syrup over the ham. Put on the lid and allow to slow cook on low for 6 to 8 hours, or cook in the oven following the recommendations on the ham's packaging.

Serves 6 to 8.

NOTE

You might think all hams would be gluten-free, but depending on where and how they are prepared and packaged, they may not be. Carefully read the labels and choose with care.

GOD BLESS AMERICA FRUIT SALAD

[BONNIE] I don't know about you, but we get a little crazy around holidays and love to make fun food that magnifies the event. This salad is more like a dessert, but the good thing about holidays is that all the rules go out the window.

3 cups strawberries, sliced

2 cups raspberries

1 cup blueberries

2 cups heavy whipping cream

½ cup C&H Baker's Sugar

1 tsp. vanilla

1 (8 oz.) pkg. cream cheese, softened

1 T. fresh lemon juice

Place all of the berries in large bowl.

In a separate bowl, whip the cream, sugar, and vanilla together until light and fluffy. In another bowl, whip together cream cheese and lemon juice and then fold in whipped cream and incorporate well. Pour cheesecake mixture over the berries and fold in carefully. Cover and refrigerate until time to serve.

Serves 6 to 8.

HOLIDAY GRAVY

[BONNIE] Growing up the daughter of an avid hunter, and with a mother who grew up raising everything they ate, meant we always had gravy for dinner. This particular gravy was saved for holidays. It's tasty but requires some time to cook, so it works perfectly for holiday cooking timetables.

Reserved giblets and neck from a turkey (if you are not a fan of giblets, it's great without)

1 T. salt

1 tsp. pepper

1 tsp. poultry seasoning

1 tsp. sage

1 to 2 cups chicken stock

2 to 3 T. cornstarch

Remove the giblets from the package and place them and the neck bone in a small saucepan. Cover the contents with water and add all of the seasonings. Bring to a boil and then reduce the heat and allow to simmer until done, approximately 30 minutes.

Remove from the heat and allow to cool (approximately another 30 minutes). Throw away the neck bone and then thinly slice the giblets. Set aside.

Pour the broth into a large skillet and add enough chicken stock to cover the bottom of the skillet and up the sides of pan to about 2 inches. Bring the broth to a boil.

In a small bowl, whisk together the cornstarch and enough chicken broth to make a lump-free slurry. Pour that carefully into the boiling broth and whisk until thickened. Reduce the heat and allow to simmer, stirring in the giblets to rewarm.

Serves 8.

NOTE

If you have picky eaters, you can make this without adding the giblets. You could use them in the Emperor's Dressing if you like.

INDEPENDENCE DAY S'MORES BARS

[BONNIE] Our family loves s'mores in any form. What a gift to figure out a dessert that would cause everyone to salivate and come together. So here we have a yummy recipe with a way to salute our country too. God bless America!

1 pkg. gluten-free chocolate sandwich cookies, crushed

½ cup (1 stick) butter, melted

1 (14 oz.) can sweetened condensed milk

7 to 10 gluten-free honey graham cracker squares, crushed

2 cups semi-sweet chocolate chips, divided

4 cups gluten-free mini marshmallows (we prefer Kraft)

2 cups red, white, and blue M&M's

Preheat the oven to 350°. Line a 13 x 9-inch baking pan with foil and then spray with a gluten-free, nonstick cooking spray.

Crush the chocolate cookies in a gallon-sized plastic bag and then pour into a mixing bowl with the melted butter, mixing thoroughly. Press into the bottom of the baking pan. Pour the condensed milk over the cookie crumbs, and then sprinkle that with the graham cracker crumbs, 1 cup of chocolate chips, and the marshmallows. Bake for 30 minutes. Remove from the oven, cover with the M&M's, and return to the oven to bake for 5 more minutes. Melt the remaining cup of chocolate chips in the microwave and drizzle over the cooling s'mores bars.

Serves 8 to 20.

LUCKY IRISH SODA BREAD

[BONNIE] Whether you're Irish or just an honorary leprechaun on Saint Patrick's Day, you are sure to enjoy this soda bread. We've always celebrated Saint Patrick's Day in the kitchen, and now that we have gluten-free options, we make enough soda bread to share with family and lucky coworkers.

Other recipes for Irish Soda Bread include caraway seeds. We never add them because they aren't something common in our spice cupboard. Just in case they are something you enjoy, we included them as an option.

4 cups 1-to-1 Namaste gluten-free flour blend

¼ cup C&H Baker's Sugar

2 tsp. baking powder

1½ tsp. baking soda

½ tsp. salt

3 T. shortening

3 T. butter, softened

½ cup raisins

1 T. caraway seeds (optional)

1¼ cups buttermilk

1 egg, lightly beaten

2 T. (¼ stick) butter, melted

Cinnamon sugar

Preheat the oven to 375°. Prepare a baking sheet with gluten-free, nonstick cooking spray.

In a large bowl, combine the flour, sugar, baking powder, baking soda, and salt and mix well. Cut in the shortening and butter until the mixture resembles coarse crumbs. Stir in the raisins and caraway seeds if you like.

In another bowl, combine the buttermilk and egg and beat together. Pour that into the crumb mixture and use a fork to combine the ingredients until the dough starts to come together.

Using your hands, knead all the ingredients into a soft dough ball. When the dough is smooth, divide it into two equal balls and place them on the baking sheet. Shape the balls into approximately 6-inch domes. Using a knife, cut a four-inch cross in the top approximately ¼ inch deep. Brush with the melted butter and sprinkle with cinnamon sugar.

Bake 40 to 45 minutes. Remove from oven, slice, and enjoy with homemade jam or apple butter while still warm. This bread is just as delicious later with a little 15-second warm-up in your microwave.

Serves 8 to 12.

NOTE

We tried this recipe with several different flour blends. This was our favorite because we didn't like the grit of rice flour or the taste of bean flour. It's a blend that's readily available online or at Costco.

~

If you don't have buttermilk on hand, pour 1¼ teaspoons
apple cider vinegar into a measuring cup and add
milk on top until you reach 1¼ cups of milk.

PECAN PIE BARS

[TAMI] Some of my favorite things, particularly around Thanksgiving and Christmas, are pecans. I know the holidays are not the only time of year they can be enjoyed, but there is just something about pecan pie, or a pumpkin pie topped with pecans, that reminds me of gatherings, fellowship, and family. This recipe dates back to early after my diagnosis. Mom developed it for me so I could feel "normal" at one of my first gluten-free Thanksgivings.

Crust

¾ cup (1½ sticks) butter, room temperature

½ cup powdered sugar

1½ cups Pamela's Products Gluten-Free Baking and
  Pancake Mix

Filling

3 eggs

2 cups pecans, coarsely chopped

1 cup sugar

1 cup light corn syrup

2 T. (¼ stick) butter, melted

1 tsp. vanilla

Preheat the oven to 350°.

Beat the butter in a large bowl until smooth. Add the sugar and beat until combined. Gradually add the flour until well mixed.

Remove the dough from the bowl and press it into an ungreased 13 x 9-inch glass pan. Bake 20 to 25 minutes or until golden brown.

In another bowl, beat the eggs with a fork, add the remaining ingredients, and mix well. Pour the filling over baked crust. Return the baking dish to the oven and bake 35 to 40 minutes or until set.

Yields 12 to 18 bars.

NOTE

When Mom originally developed this recipe, we didn't have a lot of gluten-free flour blend options. Even though there are more now, I still prefer the nutty flavor of Pamela's blend for this recipe.

PUMPKIN CAKE

[BONNIE] You've probably seen advertisements on television for dump cakes or cakes where everything is just thrown together and baked. This recipe uses a cake mix as part of the recipe, but that is where the similarities end.

Crust

2 boxes gluten-free Betty Crocker yellow cake mix (reserve 1 cup of the cake mix)

½ cup (1 stick) butter, melted

1 egg

Filling

1 (29 oz.) can pumpkin puree

2 tsp. cinnamon

1 tsp. pumpkin pie spice

½ tsp. cloves

½ cup C&H Baker's Sugar

½ cup brown sugar

⅔ cup milk

Topping

¼ cup (½ stick) butter, melted

½ cup brown sugar

1 cup pecans

Prepare a 13 x 9-inch pan by spraying it with a gluten-free, nonstick cooking spray.

In a medium bowl, combine the cake mixes (minus the reserved cup), the ½ cup melted butter, and the egg. Press into the bottom of the prepared pan.

In a large bowl, combine the pumpkin puree, spices, sugars, and milk and pour over the crust.

In a small bowl, combine the cup of reserved cake mix, melted butter, brown sugar, and pecans. Mix well until you have crumbles and then sprinkle them over the top of pumpkin filling.

Bake at 350° for 1 hour. Check to see if the center is set by inserting a knife; it should come out clean. If not, bake another 15 minutes before checking again. Serve warm.

Serves 9 to 12.

PUMPKIN CHEESECAKE BARS

[TAMI] I love pumpkin and I love cheesecake. When I was first diagnosed, my only option to enjoy either was to eat the pumpkin pie filling or cheesecake filling crustless. While this works to keep others from stealing my dessert, it's still missing something. This was one of the first recipes we created, and it still holds up. And it's delicious.

Crust

2 cups almond flour

1½ cups brown sugar

1½ tsp. cinnamon

½ cup (1 stick) butter, cold

Filling

11 oz. cream cheese, softened

1¼ cups sugar

1½ tsp. vanilla

1½ tsp. cinnamon

½ tsp. allspice

¾ cup pumpkin puree

2 eggs, slightly beaten and room temperature

Preheat the oven to 350°.

To make the crust, combine the flour, brown sugar, and cinnamon. Cut in the cold butter with a pastry cutter until the mixture resembles coarse crumbs. Press into bottom of an ungreased 13 x 9-inch pan. Bake for 15 minutes.

Cream together cream cheese, sugar, vanilla, cinnamon, and allspice in a large bowl until smooth. Beat in the pumpkin and eggs. Pour the filling over the baked crust and bake 25 to 30 minutes until set.

Yields 12 to 18 bars.

RED, WHITE, AND BLUE CHEESECAKE NIBBLES

[TAMI] My sister throws a Fourth of July barbecue every year. One year after the birth of my youngest, she asked me to bring fruit. I was determined to make it more than a typical fruit plate…it needed to be festive. I began scouring the internet for holiday-themed ideas. I kept running across cheesecakes with traditional graham cracker crusts and red, white, and blue decorations or berries on the top. To keep it gluten-free, and a side instead of a dessert, I made these. They were a hit! In fact, my sister asked me to bring them again the following year. Not only are they cute, they also are a quick and easy dish.

20 strawberries

1 cup cream cheese, softened

½ cup powdered sugar

½ to 1 tsp. almond extract

40 to 60 blueberries

Slice the strawberries in half from the top down, leaving the leaves on two equal pieces. Set the strawberries aside. In a mixing bowl, beat the cream cheese until soft and then add the powdered sugar and almond extract, beating until everything is creamed together well.

Transfer the cream cheese mixture into a piping bag or gallon-sized plastic bag. Place in the refrigerator to chill for at least ½ an hour. (This mixture can be prepared a day ahead of time and remain in the refrigerator until needed.) When ready, place the strawberries cut-side up on a platter. Pipe the cream cheese on to the cut side of the strawberries and top with 2 or 3 blueberries. These can be placed in the refrigerator for up to 2 hours or enjoyed immediately.

Serves 8 to 10.

SNOW-TOPPED CHOCOLATE MINT COOKIES

[BONNIE] These cookies are soft, chocolaty, minty pillows of loveliness. We usually make them as part of our Christmas cookie trays. If you enjoy chocolate mints, you'll want to experience these cookies.

1½ cups (187 grams) gluten-free 1-to-1 flour blend (we used Betty Crocker GF blend)

1½ tsp. baking powder

½ tsp. salt

1 (10 oz.) pkg. chocolate mint–flavored chips

¼ cup (½ stick) butter, softened

1 cup C&H Baker's Sugar
1½ tsp. vanilla
2 eggs
Powdered sugar

Preheat the oven to 350°. Line cookie sheets with parchment paper.

In a large bowl, combine the flour, baking powder, and salt.

In a double boiler, or saucepan over boiling water, melt the chocolate chips, stirring until smooth and creamy.

In another bowl, cream together the butter, sugar, and vanilla. When fluffy, add the eggs one at a time, mixing well, and then stir in the cooled chocolate. Stir in the flour mixture a little at a time until all is combined well.

Roll rounded teaspoon-sized balls of the dough in powdered sugar and place on the prepared cookie sheet. Bake for 10 to 12 minutes until the tops crack like brownie tops and allow to cool.

Yields 3 dozen cookies.

SPICED APPLE CIDER

[TAMI] This is an easy-to-make and fresh-tasting apple cider. I love putting it together early in the morning and then leaving it in the slow cooker all day—it makes the house smell great. It's one of those tastes and smells that reminds me of Christmas.

This cider warms us up when we partake in the time-honored tradition of traipsing through Christmas tree farms looking for the perfect tree with friends and family. My favorite part about this recipe is that it isn't too sweet and will have you coming back for more.

2 (128 oz.) containers apple juice (depending on size of the slow cooker)
4 to 6 cinnamon sticks
2 mandarin oranges
6 whole cloves

Pour the apple juice into the slow cooker, being careful not to fill more than ¾ full. Add the cinnamon sticks (fewer or more depending on how spicy you like your cider).

Peel the mandarin oranges and separate into slices. Stick the cloves into the orange slices before adding to the apple juice. (This way you aren't fishing out so many cloves from your mugs later.) Set the cider on low and enjoy when warm.

Serves 8 to 10.

SUCCULENT TURKEY

[BONNIE] I don't remember ever having a turkey smaller than 25 lbs. at Thanksgiving…That said, this recipe works no matter the size of the turkey. There is nothing better than a house full of people gathered to eat and celebrate the grace and provision of our heavenly Father. God bless you, friends. Enjoy the love and appreciation of your friends and family when you set this beauty in front of them.

1 (25 lb.) gluten-free turkey (check the label)

½ cup (1 stick) butter, melted

2 T. salt

1 T. pepper

1 T. poultry seasoning

1 T. sage

2 large Granny Smith apples, cored and quartered

2 large navel oranges, peeled and quartered

1 large sweet onion, peeled and quartered

3 celery stalks, halved

Remove the completely thawed turkey from its packaging and carefully flush the cavities of the bird with fresh, cool water, making sure to remove the giblets and neck bone. Place those in small saucepan and reserve to use in gravy, dressing, or broth for turkey soup. Wash off outside of the turkey and pat dry. Place in the roasting pan of your choice and brush the inside and outside of the bird with melted butter. Rub the salt and seasonings inside and out and then fill the cavities with the quartered fruits and vegetables.

Using aluminum foil, cover the turkey tent fashioned, overlapping edges to preserve heat and moisture. Place the roasting pan in the oven on the lowest rack and bake per directions on the packaging. Every hour or so, baste the turkey with the remaining butter and some of the juices from bottom of the pan, making sure to secure foil afterward.

With approximately 15 minutes to go, remove the foil and allow the bird to brown, using the last of the butter to baste. When the juices at the joint of the drumstick and breast run clean, re-cover tightly and remove from oven to rest.

Serves 8 to 20.

TWICE-BAKED SWEET POTATOES

[BONNIE] In the middle of the last century (sigh, yes, I am that old) we used to make sweet potatoes from a can and then cover them in brown sugar and marshmallows. No longer! I love sweet potatoes as a baked side with steak or chicken. And they are also wonderful with butter, a little brown sugar, and cinnamon, which serves as the base for this holiday dish.

    4 large ruby red sweet potatoes, scrubbed and eyes
      removed
    ½ cup (1 stick) butter, cut in cubes
    ½ cup brown sugar
    2 tsp. cinnamon

Preheat the oven to 375°.

Carefully pierce the sweet potato skins two or three times and then place in a microwave, making sure they are fully cooked and done in the center.

When they are ready, remove them from the microwave and cut each sweet potato in half. Place split-side up in the bottom of a 13x 9-inch glass baking dish. Spread each half with butter and then top with brown sugar and cinnamon.

Cover and bake in the oven until the butter is completely melted, and the brown sugar and cinnamon melt and blend with the potato flesh, about 20 minutes.

Serves 6 to 8.

9

KID FRIENDLY

Tasty Tidbits for Toddlers (and Kids of All Ages)

*He will yet fill your mouth with laughter
and your lips with shouts of joy.*

JOB 8:21

~

Best Caramel Corn Ever

Buttery Butter Cookies

Chocolate Butterfinger Cupcakes

Fruit Leather

Gluten-Free Playdough

Jam Thumbprint Cookies

Magic Chicken Strips

Strawberry Hand Pies

Vanilla Crescent Cookies

~

[BONNIE] When I was a child, kids were "seen and not heard" when we had guests. We even ate at the children's table until we grew up enough to be allowed to eat with the adults. The year I turned 15, I finally graduated to the adult table and was seated beside my grandmother, who wore a brand-new white pantsuit. I was terrified to make any missteps and carefully filled my plate with things that were quiet and neat, and I did not overly crowd my plate. I made sure to pass food politely and waited to be spoken to. It was going quite well, and I was down to one lowly item—cheese-stuffed celery, something I loved—but as I looked at it all alone on my plate, I knew there was no way I could eat it quietly. And I wanted to eat it so badly! I reasoned that if I carefully bent it in half, it would be half as loud when I bit down. I picked it up and carefully squeezed down, bringing the sides to the center. *Victory!* Or so I thought.

"Bonnie Jo! What have you done?"

The cheese was now clinging to the no-longer-pristine lap of my grandmother! She did forgive me…much later, I think. But the story was retold many times for years after.

Yes, our lives are all about the little loves that are part of our every waking moment. And so this final chapter includes some tidbits for those sweet little ones too.

BEST CARAMEL CORN EVER

[BONNIE] My grandma used to make this when I was younger, and she gave me the recipe when I was in high school. It was time-consuming and messy, which is why she called it popcorn goop. We used to pop it in a large pan on the stove, but as things progressed we got an air popper and then a microwave. Now yummy goodness is ready in a snap!

½ cup popcorn kernels

½ cup (1 stick) butter

1 cup brown sugar

½ cup Karo light corn syrup

½ tsp. salt

1 tsp. baking soda

1 tsp. vanilla

Air pop 12 cups of popcorn (ours makes 12 cups in one batch) and then place the popped corn in a large, unused brown grocery-sized bag.

In a large saucepan, combine the butter, brown sugar, corn syrup, and salt. Over medium heat, bring the mixture to a rolling boil. Remove from the heat and add the baking soda (this will make the mixture foam and turn a lighter brown) and vanilla, and then pour the mixture over the popcorn in the brown bag. Gather the top tightly in one hand and shake vigorously, supporting bottom of bag with your other hand.

Place the bag in the microwave and cook on high for 1 minute. Remove from microwave, shake, and return to the microwave and cook for 1 minute. Shake, return to the microwave, and cook for 1 minute. Remove and shake, repeating three more times but just for 30-second intervals. Finally, remove from microwave and spread out on two large cookie sheets to cool.

Yields 12 cups caramel corn.

BUTTERY BUTTER COOKIES

[TAMI] This fun recipe is kid-baker friendly. Recently, I had the pleasure of having my niece and nephew over, and all the kids helped me make these cookies. Each kiddo took turns adding ingredients and then helped shape and eat the cookies (and a good portion of the dough). We made it even more fun by topping the cookies with colored sugar.

> 1 cup (2 sticks) butter, softened
>
> 1 cup sugar
>
> 1 tsp. vanilla
>
> ½ tsp. almond extract (optional)
>
> 1 egg, room temperature
>
> 2⅓ cups gluten-free 1-to-1 flour blend
>
> ½ tsp. baking soda
>
> Granulated sugar or colored sugar

Heat the oven to 375°. Line a cookie sheet with waxed paper.

In a large bowl or stand mixer bowl, beat the butter until soft. Add the sugar and combine with the butter until light and fluffy. While continuing to mix, add the vanilla, almond extract if using, and the egg. Blend well. Stir in the flour and baking soda until completely incorporated.

Shape the dough into similar-sized balls—about a teaspoonful each. Place the balls on the cookie sheet 2 inches apart. Flatten with the bottom of a spoon or glass dipped in sugar (granulated or colored).

Bake 8 to 10 minutes or until set. Immediately remove from the cookie sheet to a cooling rack.

Makes approximately 4 to 5 dozen cookies.

NOTE

If you'd prefer to roll out the cookie dough, replace the 1 cup sugar with 1½ cups of powdered sugar. Duplicate the directions above to mix together the ingredients. Cover and refrigerate at least 2 hours. Divide the dough in half and roll out to a ½-inch thickness. Place the remaining half of the dough into the refrigerator to remain chilled until you are ready to shape it. Cut out with cookie cutters dipped in sugar. Transfer to waxed paper–lined cookie sheets and bake 6 to 10 minutes or until set.

CHOCOLATE BUTTERFINGER CUPCAKES

[BONNIE] Cupcakes are the favorite dessert of every person in our family under four feet (and a few above that height as well). This recipe is bound to be a favorite of the favorites for years to come because, as you know, peanut butter and chocolate are an irresistible flavor combination.

Cupcakes

1½ cups (187 grams) gluten-free 1-to-1 flour blend

½ tsp. baking powder

1 tsp. baking soda

½ tsp. salt

¾ cup Hershey's cocoa powder

1¼ cups C&H Baker's Sugar

1 cup (2 sticks) butter, room temperature

3 large eggs, room temperature

1 tsp. vanilla

¾ cup milk minus 2 T.

5 Butterfinger candy bars, chopped

Frosting

½ cup (1 stick) butter, softened

¼ cup peanut butter

5 cups powdered sugar

2 tsp. vanilla

¼ cup milk or light cream (use only enough to make a great spreading consistency)

1 cup Butterfinger candy bars, crushed

Preheat the oven to 375°. Line a muffin pan with foil muffin cups or paper cups sprayed with a spritz of gluten-free, nonstick cooking spray.

In a small mixing bowl, combine the flour, baking powder, baking soda, salt, and cocoa and whisk together until well mixed. Set aside.

In a large mixing bowl, cream together the sugar and 1 cup butter until light and fluffy, and then add eggs one at a time and the vanilla. Add one-third of the flour mix and then one-third of the milk, mixing well with each addition until all of the ingredients are combined.

Spoon the batter into the muffin cups, filling them ½ full. Sprinkle the tops with the Butterfinger bits and place in oven. Bake 18 to 20 minutes or until toothpick comes out clean. Cool completely.

While the cupcakes cool, place the butter, peanut butter, and powdered sugar in a mixing bowl and cream together. Add the vanilla and just enough milk to get the frosting to come together. Continue to mix and add milk until smooth and perfect spreading consistency.

Frost and then decorate with crushed Butterfinger bits.

Serves 6 to 12.

FRUIT LEATHER

[BONNIE] We have a food dehydrator we bought when our children were still little. Back then, every other week or so we made several trays of dried apple slices, bananas, and fruit leather. We only have two fruit leather trays, so we never made enough to last more than a day or two at most, but the kids always loved it. Fruit leather can also be made in your oven if you have eight hours at home. Basically, you puree any fresh fruit you love, add a little sugar and some fresh lemon juice, and then wait for it to dehydrate. It's simple enough little ones can help, and it tastes so good they will love it.

7 lbs. plums, berries, bananas, cherries, or any combination of fruit

¾ cup C&H Baker's Sugar

1 tsp. lemon juice

Preheat the oven to 140°. Cover cookie sheets with parchment paper sprayed with gluten-free, nonstick cooking spray.

Wash, peel, and puree the fruit in a blender or food processor. Add the sugar and lemon juice, mixing well. Pour out to an evenly spread thickness on prepared cookie sheets. Place in the oven and allow to dry for at least eight hours. The fruit leather is done when the center of the sheet is firm and no longer sticky to touch.

Remove from the oven. Using a pizza cutter, cut the fruit leather and parchment paper into strips, roll up, and store in a plastic freezer bag.

Yields approximately 16 rollups.

GLUTEN-FREE PLAYDOUGH

[TAMI] This is not edible playdough, although our dog accidentally ate a handful and suffered no ill effects. Believe it or not, store-bought playdough and all the homemade recipes we've found have contained gluten. My children have had to live without playdough until now!

Playdough is great for so many different parts of childhood and can help develop hand strength as well as hand-eye coordination. Now your family will not have to do without either. Try it. You'll love it.

2 cups water

1 cup kosher salt

2 T. alum

2 T. vegetable oil

Food coloring

2 cups gluten-free all-purpose flour

¼ cup cornstarch

In a large saucepan, combine the water, salt, alum, oil, and food coloring and heat just until the mixture is warm enough to dissolve the salt. Remove from the heat and slowly stir in the flour, mixing well to avoid lumps.

When well blended, turn out on a cornstarch "floured" board and knead well, blending in the cornstarch and smoothing out the playdough. Place in a zippered plastic bag and seal.

Yields enough playdough to make several children happy.

NOTE

When sealed in an airtight bag between uses, the playdough should last a while. It may appear to dry out, but working it in your hands will warm it back up.

We used Bob's Red Mill Gluten-Free All-Purpose Flour. It seemed to have a little more body to it than some of the other 1-to-1 flour blends. As always, we would like to encourage you to play around with the recipe, using what you are most comfortable with and finding what works for you and your family.

JAM THUMBPRINT COOKIES

[BONNIE] This is one of the first cookie recipes I let my children help me with. They loved sticking their little fingers in the balls of dough they had made. We had a lot of funny-looking cookies but, fortunately, they taste even better when you've gig-gled and made memories while crafting them. Our grandbabies love being in the kitchen now too, so we will have to try it with them soon. It is so fun to hear, "Me help stir too?"

⅔ cup (¾ stick less 1 T.) butter, room temperature

½ cup C&H Baker's Sugar

2 egg yolks

1 tsp. vanilla

½ tsp. salt

1½ cups gluten-free 1-to-1 flour blend

2 egg whites, slightly beaten

¾ cup pecans, finely chopped

⅓ cup strawberry, raspberry, or cherry jam

Preheat the oven to 350°. Spray cookie sheets with gluten-free, nonstick cooking spray.

Cream together the butter and sugar until light and fluffy. Add the egg yolks, vanilla, and salt and mix well. Gradually add the flour until it is all incorporated.

Shape the dough into ¾-inch balls, dip into the beaten egg whites, and roll in the pecans. Place on the cookie sheets and, using your thumb, slightly depress the centers of each cookie.

Bake for 15 to 17 minutes. Allow to cool and remove from the cookie sheets to cooling racks and allow to cool completely. Using a teaspoon, fill the centers with fruit jam.

Makes about 3 dozen cookies.

MAGIC CHICKEN STRIPS

[TAMI] These chicken strips were an amazing discovery one day when all I wanted were chicken fingers and fries. As you may have experienced, it can be challenging to watch your friends and family eat the gluten versions of things that you loved. My son is an extremely picky eater, and while for the most part my house is gluten-free, there are some things my gluten eaters love—for him it's Dino Bites. If you aren't familiar with Dino Bites, they are chicken nuggets shaped like dinosaurs. What a pain it was to make Dino Bites for him, chicken strips for the rest of my family, and finally grilled chicken for me. One day I tried this recipe for the whole family, and by some miracle my picky eater loves them too! The best part? This recipe is only a few ingredients and is super easy.

> 3 to 6 cups oil (so that you have at least 4 inches of oil in your Dutch oven)
>
> 4 chicken breasts, boneless and skinless
>
> 4 egg whites
>
> 2 tsp. of cornstarch
>
> Salt or pepper or taste

Heat the oil in a Dutch oven. Clean and cut the chicken breasts lengthwise into 2-inch strips.

Using a stand or hand mixer, beat the egg whites to stiff peaks. As you get close, slowly add the cornstarch and seasoning to taste.

Once the oil is heated, take one of the strips of chicken, dredge it through the egg white mixture, and gently place it in the oil as a test piece. If it rises to the top of the oil within a few seconds, the oil is ready.

Place a few pieces in the oil at a time. Fry for 2 minutes on one side and then turn them over. Once the chicken pieces are cooked all the way through, remove and place the fried chicken on a cookie sheet lined with paper towels to drain.

Serves 4.

STRAWBERRY HAND PIES

[BONNIE] One day I wanted to do something with some left-over strawberries and, as usual, was trying to think of a fun way to do something different for the grandkidlets. Hand pies are something I loved as a kid. They were a special treat, but they were never homemade. With this pie crust and filling, you'll have a fun and delicious treat to offer those you love.

Filling

  4 cups strawberries, hulled and halved

  ½ cup C&H Baker's Sugar

  2 T. cornstarch

  ¼ tsp. cinnamon

Pie Crust

  2 cups gluten-free 1-to-1 flour blend

  1 tsp. salt

  1 T. sugar

  ¾ cup (1½ sticks) butter (cut in cubes and put in freezer to chill)

  ⅓ cup shortening, very cold

  ½ cup ice water

Egg Wash and Finishing Touch

  1 egg, beaten

  1 T. water

  Sugar

Preheat the oven to 400°. Spray a cookie sheet with gluten-free, nonstick cooking spray.

Combine the strawberries, sugar, and cornstarch in a medium-sized mixing bowl and set aside.

Place the flour, salt, and sugar in a large mixing bowl and mix well to combine. With a pastry cutter, cut in the butter and shortening until the mixture resembles pea-sized crumbs. Make a well in the middle of the mixture and pour in 2 T. of the ice water and stir together with a fork. Continue to add water a tablespoon at a time just until all of the flour mixture comes together. Divide the dough in half and form two equal balls, wrap them in plastic wrap, and place in the refrigerator to chill for about 10 minutes.

Using a potato masher, mash the strawberries and then place the mixture in a small saucepan. Bring to gentle boil over medium heat until mixture thickens. Remove from the heat, stir in cinnamon, and allow to cool slightly while you shape the pie crust.

Remove one of the balls of dough from the refrigerator and place on a floured or sugared surface, rolling it out to about ¼ inch thick. Using a 3-inch biscuit cutter or overturned drinking cup, cut out an even number of crust circles. In the middle of half of the circles, place 1 to 2 T. of the strawberry puree and cover with another circle of dough. Gently fold the two crusts up and create a ⅛-inch lip. Using a fork, crimp the edges together. Make a small steam hole in the top and continue until finished with all the pies.

Place six pies on the cookie sheet. Mix the egg and water, brush the pies with the egg wash, and sprinkle with sugar. Bake until golden brown, about 30 minutes.

Makes 8 to 16 pies.

VANILLA CRESCENT COOKIES

[BONNIE] This recipe is one my father has loved for most of his life. We used to make these cookies for him if we wanted to make him feel happy or special. This recipe is easy and fun for kids to help with because working with the dough is a little like playing with clay.

    1 cup (2 sticks) butter, room temperature
    ½ cup C&H Baker's Sugar
    1 tsp. vanilla
    2 cups gluten-free 1-to-1 flour blend
    ½ tsp. salt
    2 cups pecans or walnuts, finely chopped
    1 cup powdered sugar

Preheat the oven to 400°. Line cookie sheets with parchment paper and spray with gluten-free, nonstick cooking spray.

Cream together the butter, sugar, and vanilla. Add the flour, salt, and nuts and mix well. Scoop a teaspoon-sized portion into your hand and roll into a 2-inch log that you bend in the center to create a crescent shape and place on the cookie sheet.

Bake for 10 to 12 minutes or until lightly browned, remove from oven, and carefully roll in powdered sugar.

Makes 2 to 3 dozen cookies.

CONCLUSION

Linger at our table,
laugh around our fire.
Good friends and conversations
lift our souls a little higher.

AUTHOR UNKNOWN

~

We hope and pray our cookbook has touched you and your family's heart, and given you hope and the tools you need to tackle gluten-free cooking. If you have celiac disease, we know your concerns firsthand and understand the angst involved in trying to cook for others while staying healthy. We hope we have provided you with a well-rounded look at living gluten-free along with love and laughter that will feed your spirit as well.

GLUTEN-FREE

Get All the Details

She is like the merchant ships, bringing her food from afar.

PROVERBS 31:14

~

'Tis an ill cook who cannot lick his own fingers.

WILLIAM SHAKESPEARE

~

[BONNIE] Until you have been given a diagnosis that requires a gluten-free diet, you might never understand how much of the world of food is saturated in gluten or products that contain gluten. I'm sure the woman in Proverbs 31 was no stranger to pitfalls of the marketplace in her day.

In fact, she has long been my hero, and, if I'm honest, the kind of woman I have yet to come close to in practice. When I was a young mother with three toddlers, this verse seemed so old fashioned that I breezed past it. After all, I had trouble getting us all ready at the same time to go to the corner grocery. Later, though, after Tami was diagnosed with celiac disease, it rang true, and we found ourselves so thankful for the internet and being able to find products not yet available in our hometown.

Likewise, to William Shakespeare's point, as a teenager I thought he was writing about my little brother, who used to throw leftovers together to create the most unbelievable meals. Now this quote means so much more. If you have celiac disease, which is a lifelong condition with no reprieve, you have to be careful of everything that touches your lips, hands, and even nostrils. If it's necessary for you to eat gluten-free to live, or if you choose to eat gluten-free as a healthier option, Tami and I will try to give you some helpful insights.

What Is Celiac Disease?

The Celiac Disease Foundation has this information on their website (celiac.org):

> Celiac disease is a serious autoimmune disorder that can occur in genetically predisposed people where the ingestion of gluten leads to damage in the small intestine. It is estimated to affect 1 in 100 people worldwide. Two and one-half million Americans are undiagnosed and are at risk for long-term health complications.
>
> When people with celiac disease eat gluten, their body mounts an immune response that attacks the small intestine. These attacks lead to damage on the villi, small fingerlike projections that line the small intestine and promote nutrient absorption. When the villi get damaged, nutrients cannot be absorbed properly into the body.
>
> Celiac disease is hereditary, meaning that it runs in families. People with a first-degree relative with celiac disease (parent, child, sibling) have a 1 in 10 risk of developing celiac disease.*

[Tami] Gluten is a protein found in wheat, rye, barley, some oats, and many things derived from them. (A hidden example would be modified food starch.) When I eat something with gluten, I feel very sick for several days.

Other Reasons to Eat Gluten-Free

[Tami] There are a variety of health reasons to eat gluten-free, and there are differences between celiac disease, a gluten allergy, and gluten intolerance or gluten sensitivity.

While preparing to write this chapter about the differences between separate reactions to ingesting gluten, I realized I knew several people who fall into each one of these categories—people who eat gluten-free cover a wide spectrum, from those who choose the lifestyle for personal reasons to those who have severe reactions when even the slightest amount of gluten comes in contact with their food.

First, let's begin with gluten allergies and allergic reactions. They can be as mild as hives but can also include people who have anaphylactic reactions to

---

* https://celiac.org/celiac-disease/understanding-celiac-disease-2/what-is-celiac-disease.

wheat. The same range exists within the group who suffer from dermatitis her-petiformis. It resembles eczema, but in someone else may be misdiagnosed as herpes. Similar to celiac disease, individuals with dermatitis herpetiformis can manage their symptoms by removing gluten from their diet.*

Another group ranges from gluten- or wheat-sensitive individuals. It has always been believed that those with gluten or wheat sensitivity do not suffer damage to their small intestines. However, in a July 2016 study, researchers at Columbia University Medical Center released findings that, while incon-clusive, showed gluten-sensitive people may actually be damaging their small intestines in the same way as those with celiac disease, but to a lesser degree.†

Gluten sensitivities can manifest themselves in so many different symp-toms that they may not even seem to be connected to your diet. If you have symptoms such as diarrhea, nausea, or migraines after eating breads or pasta, you would probably make the connection, but if you become moody or your joints ache, you might not. These symptoms can all be related, though medi-cal testing is required to know for sure. A way to be proactive would be to keep a food and symptom journal prior to seeing your doctor.

I have friends who have chosen a gluten-free lifestyle not because of a med-ical diagnosis, but because they found that eating gluten-free alleviated several seemingly unrelated symptoms. Some of those symptoms included inflam-mation in their joints, continual fatigue, ADHD behavior, and even autism.

Whether you are trying out a gluten-free diet to see if it fits into your life-style or you have allergies, sensitivities, celiac disease, or dermatitis herpeti-formis, our hope is that this lifestyle will not inhibit your life but can become an adventure!

How to Avoid Cross Contamination

[Tami] Once when my family and I were at a restaurant, and after I had explained to the waiter that I had celiac disease, I received my meal with bread on top of my steak! I had to send it back. Enough time elapsed that we thought surely they had made a new meal, but instead they must have just replated it because we didn't even leave the restaurant before I was ill and then in bed for the next three days.

Cross contamination is the most difficult aspect of celiac for non-sufferers to grasp, and most people wouldn't give a second thought to just taking the

---

* https://celiac.org/celiac-disease/understanding-celiac-disease-2/dermatitis-herpetiformis.

† http://newsroom.cumc.columbia.edu/blog/2016/07/26/columbia-researchers-find-biological-explanation-wheat-sensitivity-2.

roll off the steak and handing it back. However, for someone with celiac, inadvertently ingesting a crumb of something with gluten in it or even breathing in wheat flour that dusts up into the air can cause illness. When baking for family gatherings, we rely heavily on the ideas listed below. They may sound extreme, but making sure everyone has a happy, healthy meal makes them worthwhile.

I remember when I was first diagnosed and trying to share with the family all these different ideas at once. I was met with disbelief and shock. Not only was I asking for some extreme undertakings, but back then celiac wasn't as widely understood as it is now. It wasn't until I had my first cross contamination episode while at a family event that people began to understand what I'd been saying. I hope you can learn from my experience and ease people in.

Here are some of our cross contamination "hacks" to help you stay healthy:

- Toasters are gluten hotbeds. Toaster Bags can help solve this problem, but you may want to invest in a gluten-free toaster. (This goes double for waffle irons!)

- Shared wooden spoons, wooden cutting boards, and wooden rolling pins can all cause cross contamination. Buying separate utensils and marking them, or buying plastic, was our solution.

- Don't buy matching toothbrushes! Enough said.

- Don't share straws even with your most adorable little love bugs! One of the hardest things to deal with. Kiddos need to learn to share—but you don't!

- Mayonnaise, peanut butter, butter, and jam are all suspect unless you marked GF ones for your use only. Ask anyone bringing a mayonnaise-based salad or dessert with peanut butter to please use an unopened jar. Squeeze mayo also works great!

- Chip bags can cause a problem too. Pour from the bag rather than reaching directly into the bag or when sharing with someone eating gluten.

- Salad bars are problematic. Even if it seems mostly safe, watch the people at the salad bar for about five minutes. You'll change your mind. You never know what gluten lurks there!

- Potlucks can be stressful when considering what could be contaminated. Ask if you can go through the line first, and be sure to bring something you know is safe.

- Candy dishes or communal bowls…yikes! Wrapped candy can be a better solution there. Otherwise, avoid at all costs.

- Pizza stones and seasoned skillets can hold gluten. You need to give these away or clearly mark what is gluten-free.

I hope this brief list will help you avoid some of the learning opportunities I found myself in the last few years. As I said before, it can be hard at the beginning of your gluten-free journey. Be understanding but firm! You are entitled to healthy eating just like everyone else. Feel free to share this list and other parts of this book with anyone who may be having a hard time understanding. Those who love you will come around, though you may have to be willing to supply your own food for a while. I hope you found some appealing ideas for family gatherings in this book.

Other Names for Gluten

Sometimes it isn't obvious what might contain gluten. Read labels and try to pick foods labeled gluten-free to be 100 percent safe. In a pinch, here are a few things to watch out for:

Barley malt	Graham—flour and crackers (unless labeled gluten-free)	Natural flavoring
Bouillon cubes		Ramen noodles
Bran		Soy sauce (unless labeled gluten-free)
Bulgur	Malt—vinegar, flavoring, and syrup	
Caramel—color or flavoring		Tabbouleh
Farina	Matzo	Udon
Food starch	Modified food starch	Vegetable starch
		Wheat starch

Some cheeses are not gluten-free. Any cheese made with mold spores can be a hidden danger because most mold spores are started on bread.

~

Ways of labeling hidden gluten is ever-changing and evolving. The Gluten Intolerance Group has a lot of helpful information they update frequently. Be sure to check out their website at gluten.org.

> *I am the LORD your God who takes hold of*
> *your right hand and says to you,*
> *Do not fear; I will help you.*

ISAIAH 41:13

CONVERSION TIPS

Gluten to Gluten-Free

~

Sometimes baking or cooking gluten-free isn't a simple 1-to-1 conversion because of the differing nature of the gluten-free ingredients. You can use these conversion tips to quickly convert some of your favorite gluten recipes. If the gluten recipe calls for…

- 1 tsp. baking soda, use 1 tsp. baking soda and ½ tsp. baking powder.
- 1 tsp. baking powder, use 1½ tsp. baking powder.
- 1 egg, use 2 eggs and reduce liquid in recipe by 2 T.
- 2 eggs, use 3 eggs and reduce liquid by 2 T.
- 1 cup of flour, use 125 grams of a gluten-free 1-to-1 flour blend.
- Add an extra egg white before baking if your dough is too dry.
- Consider swapping buttermilk for milk for a richer texture.
- Consider swapping brown sugar for granulated sugar to add moisture to your dough.

OUR FAVORITE GLUTEN-FREE FOOD PRODUCTS

~

[TAMI] Two of the main messages I hope you received from this book are:

1. "Don't be afraid to try new things!"

2. "Give yourself (and the gluten-free manufacturing community) some grace and have fun with the adventure!"

Great Options to Consider

Because new products are constantly coming out, our favorites are constantly changing.

- Annie's Gluten-Free Macaroni & Cheese
- Barilla Gluten-Free Elbows
- Barilla Gluten-Free Penne
- Best Foods Real Mayonnaise
- Betty Crocker Gluten-Free 1-to-1 Rice Flour Blend
- Betty Crocker gluten-free cakes, cookies, and brownie mixes
- Bob's Red Mill Gluten-Free 1 to 1 Baking Flour

- Bob's Red Mill Gluten-Free All-Purpose Baking Flour
- Bob's Red Mill Gluten-Free Classic Oatmeal
- Bob's Red Mill Stone Ground White Rice Flour
- Bob's Red Mill Xanthan Gum
- Chex cereals from General Mills
- Foster Farms Smart Choices Gluten-Free Breast Strips

- Franz gluten-free breads and buns
- Hershey's Unsweetend Cocoa
- Kettle brand chips
- Kinnikinnick Donuts
- Krusteaz Gluten-Free Blueberry Muffin Mix
- Krusteaz Gluten-Free Double Chocolate Brownie Mix
- Lay's potato chips
- Maseca Gluten-Free Instant Yellow Corn Masa Flour
- McCormick Original Taco Seasoning Mix
- Mission Corn Tortilla Chips
- Ortega Taco Seasoning
- Pam's Original Cooking Spray (be sure to check the label)
- Prego Farmers' Market Classic Marinara Sauce
- Quaker Select Starts Gluten-Free Instant Oatmeal—Maple & Brown Sugar
- Simple Truth Gluten-Free Waffles
- Tostitos Original (corn tortilla chips)
- Udi's gluten-free breads
- Udi's Gluten-Free Thin & Crispy Pizza Crusts

The really nice thing about these products is they are all yummy—even for family members who don't have to eat gluten-free. Today we can be more spontaneous because we no longer have to prepare everything from scratch.

What Does Certified Gluten-Free Mean?

When a product has been given the GF logo, it means that it has been certified gluten-free. To earn this logo, the manufacturing of gluten-free goods must meet strict quality and purity guidelines. Their products are tested to ensure that they are free of gluten and cross contamination within tolerance levels. There have been multiple studies that prove even the people with the most severe cases of celiac disease or dermatitis herpetiformis can withstand a minuscule amount of gluten, and all products must remain below this threshold—less then 10 parts per million (ppm) to be certified gluten-free.

Within the United States we have such strict labeling laws that a product cannot be labeled gluten-free unless it meets these standards. When buying products from other countries, be sure to read all labels carefully, and when in doubt, contact the manufacturers. The GF logo has been tremendously helpful in making grocery shopping just a bit easier.

HELPFUL BAKING TOOLS

~

B elow is a list of the tools we used when trying out the recipes in this book. We tried hard to use what we already had in our kitchens, but we found in some instances that buying the right tool for the job made a *big* difference. We do not make recommendations lightly. Over the years, we've read cookbooks, online sources, and dietician sources that insisted new baking tools and novelty appliances were necessary to live gluten-free. We don't agree, but here are some items we did find helpful. Remember, they're only useful if they work for you and your cooking/baking lifestyle.

- *Food scale.* A good, digital scale is so helpful when you are looking to convert your own family favorites.

- *Plastic cutting boards and spoons.* Your previously used wooden spoons and cutting boards actually trap gluten. Out with the old, in with the new!

- *Mini food processor.* This little gizmo is fantastic for making salsas, sauces, and pesto.

- *Stand and/or hand mixer.* We love our stand mixers and have had them for years. If you don't have one, a hand mixer will work just fine.

- *Toaster bags.* These handy bags are great for keeping your toast, sandwiches, and other items contamination free and also nice and warm.

- *Foil muffin tin liners.* Gluten-free baked goods tend to be moist and sticky. We've found the foil muffin liners sprayed with gluten-free, nonstick cooking spray work best for gluten-free muffins and cupcakes—and they look pretty too.

- *Parchment paper.* Parchment paper will help to keep your gluten-free baked goods from burning.

- *Gluten-free griddle.* Only use gluten-free recipes with this griddle.

- *Gluten-free tortilla press.* Seriously, you'll soon become a master at making your own tortillas. They are so much fun! And delicious.

- *Glute-free waffle iron.* What is better than a Saturday morning with waffles topped with your favorite things? Dedicate this little device to your breakfast enjoyment.

QUICK BAKING TIPS

~

1. Give yourself grace. Gluten-free baking is tough but not impossible. Don't give up the first time something doesn't turn out right. Keep trying!

2. Don't be afraid if gluten-free batter looks wetter then you are used to. I've learned that gluten-free baking mixes can dry out easily, and so moist batter is almost essential to not have a dry result.

3. Stick to the recipe the first time you try a new gluten-free dish. Gluten-free baking can be a little tricky and may have slightly different steps or ingredients than you are used to. Give yourself a baseline before you make changes so you can decide if you like the changes or if you like the original recipe.

4. When using some of the wonderful boxed mixes available now, add a teaspoon of vanilla to help it taste more homemade.

5. Spray muffin papers or muffin tins no matter how wet the batter is with a gluten-free, nonstick cooking spray. Gluten-free batters tend to leave some of the baked goods behind in the tin or muffin papers. A cupcake or muffin can come out perfectly if you spray it first.

6. Especially when baking gluten-free cookies, line your baking pans and sheets with parchment paper. In my experience, gluten-free cookies and cakes tend to burn on the bottoms *a lot* quicker than similar gluten containing recipes.

7. When changing your kitchen over from gluten to gluten-free, wooden utensils and cutting boards are NOT your friend. Time to go shopping!

NOT IN THE MOOD TO COOK?

Tips and Tricks for Eating Out

~

Let's face it. Eating gluten-free at home is hard enough, but it can be really scary to trust someone else to make your food, especially if you have a medical reason to be gluten-free. What I've included here are my quick tips and tricks for eating out. Each one of these tips has a story that illustrates the point further. If you'd like to read the sometimes-comical situations I've gotten myself into, feel free to check out my blog, glutenfreelifehacks.com.

- You are your only full-time advocate. Don't feel shy. Stay strong for your health!

- Don't be afraid to ask. If you have a sense of shame, it's time to lose it or you're going to miss out on some amazing food and experiences.

- When someone at a restaurant helps you navigate what may or may not be gluten-free, go out of your way to show gratitude and appreciation.

- Don't be afraid to take food to someone else's house if it enables you to eat or have a similar meal. Check with your hosts about ways you can help alleviate their stress by providing a gluten-free option yourself.

Appendix G

HOLIDAY MENUS

~

CONNECT WITH TAMI

I have a blog where I post about gluten-free life hacks. I would love for you to visit it. I include pictures and share about the sometimes-comical situations I find myself in while living gluten-free in a gluten-filled world. I would also love to hear from you and discover some of the tips and tricks you've learned in your journey. Please feel free to visit me at **glutenfreelifehacks.com**.

INDEX

~

NOTES

NOTES

To learn more about Harvest House books and
to read sample chapters, visit our website:

www.harvesthousepublishers.com

HARVEST HOUSE PUBLISHERS
EUGENE, OREGON